LOOKING BACK
AT THE
1950s

A Trip Down Memory Lane

Picture Credits

UK Photo and History Archive, Alamy, Jean and Robert Freeman, Steve Freeman, Beverley Riddle, Heather and Bob Shorthouse, Beryl and Norman Hale.

Published by Britain on Film Books

Printed by Book Printing UK www.bookprintinguk.com

Remus House, Coltsfoot Drive, Peterborough, PE2 9BF

Printed in Great Britain

ISBN 978-1-80352-693-5

Contents

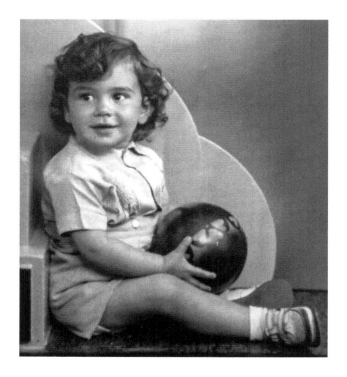

The author aged about one. Unfortunately for my parents I didn't grow into the angelic child this photo might suggest.

David Hale is a post-war baby boomer who grew up in the 1950s. Over the past 20 years he has written extensively about Britain during the 20th century and has now turned his attention to the decade of his childhood.

"The past is a foreign country: they do things differently there."
L.P. Hartley, 1953.

Introduction
****

If you remember coal fires, waking up with ice on the inside of windows, the tin bath, Andy Pandy, the children's matinee on Saturday morning, hanging out in the Milk Bar, National Service, the mangle and the washing dolly, school milk, or playing marbles or hopscotch in the street, then you were probably around in the 1950s. And if that's the case, 'Looking Back At The 1950s' will take you on a nostalgic trip down Memory Lane, as it recalls the joys and challenges of growing up in post-war Britain and offers a glimpse into a world that has long since vanished.

David Hale skilfully combines his own memories of growing up in the fifties, historical insights, evocative photos of the age, news reports, and humorous observations to paint an entertaining and heart-warming look back at life in 1950s Britain.

December 31, 1949

Tonight, the 'Frightful Forties' — years of war in its most terrible form and of immeasurable human suffering end, unhonoured and unsung.

It is natural to ask, at the present moment, not only what the coming year will bring, but what the fifties will have to inscribe on the pages of history.

Childhood
****

Primary School

While many aspects of life have changed dramatically since the 1950s, the domination of school in children's lives has remained constant over the decades, mind you, kids today might have things a little easier than we did back then. Take our first day at infant school for example. For many of us this was a traumatic experience as it was our first time away from our mothers. There was no pre-school back then to break us in gently and that first day could be a tearful occasion for both child and mother. Another big difference was that most of us walked to school, whatever the weather. Even after a heavy snowfall schools stayed open and there was no excuse for not attending. I remember waking up one morning to deep snowdrifts half the height of the front door.

We had to dig our way out and I arrived at school freezing cold and soaking wet, along with most of the other kids.

The school day started with assembly when the pupils trooped into the school hall in their class groups, sat on the floor in lines and pretended to listen to what the head teacher had to say. We sang a hymn, said the Lord's Prayer, and trooped off again to start our lessons.

The teaching agenda was dominated by the 'Three R's', reading, writing and arithmetic, which were considered the basic skills we needed to get by.

Most 50s primary school pupils will remember the whole class chanting the times tables out loud, over and over, until we knew them by heart – that was the idea anyway.

The Ink Monitor

Neat handwriting was another vital tool in a child's armoury and was practiced daily, at first with a pencil, and table top sharpeners were a feature of every classroom. When we reached the grand old age of about seven, we were considered old enough to be let loose with a pen, usually basic ones with wooden handles and metal nibs. These required access to a supply of ink and most fifties school children will remember the wooden desks with lift up tops and small holes in the top for an inkwell. The important job of filling the inkwells fell to the ink monitor.

This was a privileged position that was usually bestowed as a reward for good behaviour.

If you were lucky enough and the school allowed it, you might have had your very own fountain pen, a Parker if your parents could afford it, but more likely a Platignum, along with a bottle of Quink.

School Milk

The status of ink monitor was equalled only by that of the milk monitor, whose job it was to distribute the little bottles of milk that were forced on us daily, and are an abiding memory for most children of the 50s.

In 1945, the Labour Government passed the Free School Milk Act, which gave every child under 18 the right to a third of a pint of milk every day.

With food rationing in force, the idea was to supplement the child's diet, a noble cause, but one that was detested by almost every child in the country. It wasn't too bad in the colder months, (except when it froze solid and poked the tops off), but in the summer, when it was warm and the cream curdled, it was quite disgusting.

Mind you, whether you loved or loathed school milk, there were compensations. With a flick of the fingers and a little imagination, the foil milk bottle tops made great flying saucers.

Physical Education

PE also became an
essential part of the
school curriculum in the
fifties. There was no gym
kit, and it was done in
vest, knickers or pants,
and bare feet, or a pair of
black pumps from Wool-
worths if you were lucky.

Baby Boomers

Fifties kids were a product of the huge increase in the
number of births that followed the end of the Second
World War, the baby boomers as they were known.
This meant that school class sizes in the 1950s were
large, with often thirty to forty children per class.
Classroom assistants hadn't yet been invented so it was
down to the teacher alone to enforce discipline, and,
by today's standards, it could be brutally administered.
Sitting with your hands on your head might be the pun-
ishment for a minor transgression, and a rap across the
knuckles or on the backside with a ruler for more serious
breaches was common.

The only teacher I can remember from primary school is Miss Fowler, and for all the wrong reasons.

Miss Fowler was particularly fond of using her ruler to punish even the slightest breach of discipline and I was terrified of her; so terrified that I once wet myself in class rather than ask to go to the toilet.

I bet many of you remember you own Miss Fowler!

The Nit Nurse

The 1950s brought a revolution in health care for children, with much of it targeted at schools. There were routine eye and hearing tests, and of course, regular checks by the nit nurse for head-lice.

The whole class lined up to have their hair combed carefully with a nit comb to check for infestation.

None of this was particularly unpleasant and offered a welcome break from chanting '2 x 2 is 4' etc, but when the day came for the polio jab it was a different story. Children lined up with their left arms hanging free from jumpers and watching classmates receive the jab.

Apprehension mounted as you got nearer to the front of the queue until, oh no, it was your turn.

I'm obviously glad of the protection that injection gave me, but the sensation of the big needle going into my arm has stayed with me and given me a life-long dread of injections. I've had them when it was necessary but, before each one, I'm back in that queue with my arm hanging out of my jumper.

Does anyone else feel like that or am I just a wimp?

The Eleven Plus Exam

When children reached the grand old age of eleven, they faced the Eleven plus, a compulsory exam that would decide the next stage of their education and potentially their whole future. Those who passed the exam had the chance to go to grammar school where the academic curriculum was geared to achieving 'O' and 'A' Levels, a place at university and a professional career.

It was standard practice for parents that could afford it to pay for private tuition for their children to increase their chances of a grammar school place, and a bribe of a new bike was not uncommon.

The only option for those who failed the exam was to attend the local secondary modern, where the education was heavily biased towards technical and vocational subjects to churn out the future plumbers, carpenters, typists, nurses, factory workers and shop workers.

Of course, there were secondary school pupils who exceeded the expectations of the system and achieved great success, but it was largely down to their own determination and effort rather than the education system.

While secondary modern schools were mixed, grammar schools were divided into boys and girl's schools so that students would concentrate on learning without the distraction of the opposite sex. Even the teachers were segregated, with male teachers at the boy's school and female at the girls.

The education also differed. Part of the role of a girl's grammar school was to train the pupils to become perfect middle-class wives to the bank managers, doctors, lawyers, and accountants being churned out at the boy's school. Domestic Science was the programme of lessons that would produce these exemplary specimens of middle-class womanhood. Girls were taught how to how to cook, how to lay a table for a dinner party, how to sew and darn and embroider, even how to iron a man's shirt (collar and cuffs first girls, don't forget)

There are some memories though, that most senior school pupils will share, girls and boys. Who can forget the unique, gassy smell of the science classroom, or being let loose with a razor-sharp scalpel on a dead frog or a cow's eyeball.

How did you do in the Eleven Plus?

Whether you passed or failed, on page 145 is an opportunity to re-sit the exam all over again with questions from a 1950s Eleven Plus paper, and be warned, you might find it harder than you expect.

The answers are on page 152.
A score of just over 70% will count as a pass, and no cheating please. Give yourself a rap on the knuckles with a ruler if you do!

IN THE NEWS
1950

January 26, 1950

The Independent Sovereign Republic of India is being formally proclaimed. India has chosen to be a republic, and Pakistan a Dominion.
But both remain in the Commonwealth as partners in that galaxy of free peoples.

March 17, 1950

TIMOTHY JOHN EVANS EXECUTED

Timothy John Evans of Rillington Place. Notting Hill, Kensington, 25-year-old lorry driver, was executed at Pentonville prison last week.

He was sentenced to death at the Old Bailey on January 13 for the murder of his daughter Geraldine, aged 14 months. He had pleaded not guilty.

Police stated at the trial that they searched Evan's home and found the strangled bodies of his wife and daughter in the wash house

Playtime
****

Do you remember the stampede to get into the play-ground when the bell rang?
After being stuck in the classroom it was such a relief to be out and free.

In the longer break at dinnertime (there was no such thing as lunch back then) the playground was glorious mayhem. Footballs and skipping ropes appeared as if from nowhere and groups of kids ran around madly trying to avoid being tagged.

Eeny, meeny, miny, mo.

Before you could start a game of tag somebody had to be picked to be it, or on, which could be decided with a simple rhyme such as "eeny, meeny, miny, mo."
This is one of those rhymes that's ingrained in our subconscious - once we hear the first word, the rest roll out unprompted, and if you've ever used the rhyme, you have something in common with a lot of other humans. The simple rhyme is familiar to almost every English speaker on the planet. So what is the origin of this meaningless combination of words that is known to so many people?
It's thought it may have started in primitive times as a simple way for uneducated people to count. For example, a shepherd could point at his sheep one by one and repeat "eeny, meeny, miny, mo" dropping a pebble into a sack on each repetition. At the end he would have an accurate estimate of how many sheep were in his flock.

For us kids, there were other ways of deciding who was on, some more elaborate than eeny, meeny, like the one my pals and I used.

We stood in a tight circle and all put one foot forward next to each others while one of the group chanted; "Your shoes need cleaning, please change your foot," at the same time pointing at the feet in turn in time with the words. Whoever's foot the saying ended on swapped feet and if it ended on them again, they were out. This continued until only one person was left and he or she would be 'it'.

I can understand the need of a Bronze-Age shepherd to count his sheep, but Lord only knows why we went to such elaborate lengths to start a simple game of tag, but that's with hindsight. At the time we took the ritual very seriously, after all, when you're young, play is a serious business, take marbles for example.

Marbles

Marble time is here

ONE sign that "the time of the singing of birds" is not far off is when boys bring out their marbles and turn street gutters into a track for the testing of skill. I saw half-a-dozen boys the other night ushering in the marble season in Baker Street.

Who decides when "marley" time (as it used to be called in my native county when I was a boy) should start? As far as I know it is an unsolved mystery. But start it does, as if to a starter's pistol.

Yes, there really was a marble season when, for a few weeks every year, schools up and down the country were gripped by marble fever. Marble season was never advertised yet without fail, every year, it sprang into life quite spontaneously and it seems that this might be a custom with a very long history. Old records show that in medieval times, marbles was traditionally played between Ash Wednesday and midday on Good Friday after which, playing marbles would bring bad luck.

Although we knew nothing of its tradition, we looked forward to the marble season with eager anticipation, but things didn't always go to plan.

I remember breaking my right arm just before the start of one marble season; a disaster as I was right-handed, but I was determined to take part and decided to play with my left hand, which was a big mistake!

I lost all my marbles on the first day of the season, every single one. I was distraught and spent the rest of the season as a jealous spectator.

Marbles is played all over the world and is one of the oldest games known to man. There is evidence that it was played by our Stone Age ancestors with small round pebbles.

What did you call yours?

The language of marbles is almost as colourful as the marbles themselves and depended on where in the country you lived.

Standard size marbles could be marlies or taws. In the north of England a large marble was a 'bottle-washer', elsewhere 'a biggie' 'a boulder' 'a bonker' 'a masher' 'a dobber' or 'a toebreaker'.

There were also 'aggies' 'bumblebees' 'catseyes' 'oilies' 'steelies', and so on, to describe the appearance of the marble. There were also all sorts of thrilling games we could play with them.

Probably the simplest game you could play with marbles involved two players, one of whom tossed a marly, which the other tried to hit with his. This game could be played almost anywhere, including the gutter.

In rural parts of England this was known as a going-to-school game because it could be played on the way to school - if you set out early enough that is!

Another popular game was Ring Taw, in which marbles are placed in a circle on the ground and shot at with the aim of knocking them out of the circle. Any marble displaced is kept by the player who knocks it out.

When there are no more marbles in the circle the game is over, and the winner is whoever collected the most.

My personal favourite took place in the school play-ground where the surface was even.

A boy, (they were nearly always boys for some reason) would line up several marbles next to each other – these could be touching or with spaces in between – and shooters would aim at the line of marbles from a set number of paces away.

This was determined by how many marbles were in the line, for example, if there were five marbles, the distance to aim from was 5 paces. The boy making the line, let's call him the shouter, would invite others to aim at it by shouting; "five marlies from five paces."

If the shooter hit the line he kept the marbles, but if he missed, he lost his own. There were usually several shouters next to each other with different offers and all shouting the odds, just like bookies at a racecourse trying to attract customers: "four marlies from four paces," "ten marlies from ten paces."

If competition was stiff there could be a special offer, like "eight marlies from seven paces." And sometimes there were challenges that really attracted attention, such as "fifty marlies from fifty paces".

When these were called, a large crowd gathered to watch the spectacle.

Conkers

Another game with a season, this time for obvious reasons, was conkers.

As soon as the horse chestnuts started to ripen, groups of boys gathered round the trees throwing sticks into the branches to bring down what they hoped would be a prize specimen.

The game of conkers was first played using snail shells or hazelnuts, but in 1848 we have the first recorded game using horse chestnuts taking place on the Isle of Wight. It grew in popularity and by the end of the 19th century was played everywhere horse chestnuts grew.

In 1965, the first World Conker Championships took place in Ashton, Northamptonshire and still take place in October every year with hundreds of competitors from all over the world. For the first 10 years, all of the champions were British until, shock horror, in 1976, the Mexican, Jorge Ramirez Carrillo, defeated the reigning champion in the final.

As we all know, if you want a conker with the potential to become a champion, it should come straight from the tree rather than windfall, but there were a number of tricks to enhance the natural properties of the horse chestnuts and therby, make them more effective weapons.

Soaking them in vinegar or baking them in the oven were two of the most common, but some fanatics kept conkers collected the previous year, which was said to make them harder and more dense.

It all sounds like cheating if you ask me and something I would never resort to – well, almost never. When we felt our conkers were ready to take into battle, all that was left to do was to make a hole– using a meat skewer as I recall – thread a string through the hole, tie a knot in the string, and head off in search of opponents.

The point of the game was to take it in turns to try to smash your rival's conker to bits, and it didn't half hurt if you got rapped on the knuckles by a poorly aimed shot.

If you emerged victorious you could call your conker a 'one-er'. Another victory would make it a 'two-er' and so on. In other parts of the country they became, colonels, kings and emperors based on the number of victories.

Polly on the Mopstick or Bung the Bucket.

This was a game for two teams that began with a member of one team standing with his back against a sturdy object, like a tree or a wall, while the rest bent into a leapfrog posture, one behind the other. The other team then proceeded, one by one, to leap on to the backs of their opponents. If the first team bore the combined weight of all the second teams players, they were victorious, but if they collapsed, they were the losers.

British Bulldog

What a great way to let off steam British Bulldog was- if you didn't mind a few cuts and grazes, bumps and bruises that is! One player was chosen to be the bulldog, by as elaborate and long-winded process as possible, obviously.

The others ran from one side of the allotted space to the other without being rugby tackled, tripped, or stopped by any other means by the bulldog. Those that were caught became bulldogs themselves until only one player remained, and he or she was declared the winner.

Skipping

Rough and tumble games like British Bulldog were played mainly by boys. The girls meanwhile, were usually engaged in more imaginative, creative past times, like skipping for example.

Skipping could be a simple enough activity involving one person and a piece of rope but could also be a complex game with several players. The rope, often an old washing line, was turned by a player at each end.

When the rope was turning smoothly, one or more skippers joined in, jumping over the rope as it touched the ground and, if they were feeling energetic, performing kicks, sizzlers, splits or other amazing tricks as they jumped.

If their weren't enough skippers to allocate one to each end of the rope to turn it, the other end could be secured to an available lamp post, or if you were really desperate, you could always recruit little brother. While they were a nuisance most of the time, as we can see, they did occasionally have their uses.

The skipping was often done to the rhythm of a song or chant performed by all those who weren't in the rope at the time, with players changing places in specific parts of the song. Do you remember this one?

I had a little puppy
His name was Tiny Tim
I put him in the bathtub, to see if he could swim
He drank all the water, he ate a bar of soap
The next thing you know he had a bubble in his throat
In came the doctor (player jumps in)
In came the nurse (player jumps in)
In came the lady with the alligator purse (player jumps in)
Out went the doctor (player jumps out)
Out went the nurse (player jumps out)
Out went the lady with the alligator purse (player jumps out)

As a young boy I remember being in awe of the girls performing these mesmerising moves. This only increased when they occasionaly let me join in, and I made a complete fool of myself. Although, most of the girls couldn't kick a ball for toffee, so I suppose there's some justice in the world.

Cat's Cradle

An equally impressive game played predominantly by girls was Cat's Cradle, or Jack in the Pulpit, as it is sometimes known.

All that was needed to play the game was a piece of string or wool and a lot of practice. To the untrained eye, the participants were just wrapping their hands up in string, but what was really happening was poetry in motion. The speed of the hand and finger movements was bewildering until, suddenly, from the complicated tangle, emerged a butterfly, a rabbit, or even the Eiffel Tower.

Jacks or Five Stones

This was another game of dexterity played with a collection of small objects that are thrown into the air and caught in a variety of ways. The game is played all over the world and its origins stretch back into the stone age, when small animal bones were used

Hopscotch

While games like skipping and Cats Cradle were mainly played by girls, and less skilful ones like British Bulldog by boys, there were some games that brought us together – hopscotch for example.

Who didn't love a game of hopscotch? All you needed to produce hours of fun was a piece of chalk, enough space to mark out the court, and a flat stone or some other suitable object to use as a marker.

I'm sure most people who grew up in the fifties will also remember Farmers in his Den and What's the time Mr Wolf, which were both games everyone could join in. How tension mounted as we got closer to Mr Wolf. knowing that his dinnertime was imminent.

As well as all these structured games to play, there were other activities that just seemed to happen spontaneously. Playing football – with jumpers for goal posts of course; a cricket match in the street with a dustbin lid for wickets; tying ropes to lamp posts to make a swing; (the old fashioned lamp posts were perfect for that weren't they); making daisy chains;

doing handstands against the wall, (remembering to tuck your dress into your knickers); building dens; or being cowboys and Indians. So much to do, and not a computer in sight!

Or you could scrump apples from Mr Robinson's garden. The funny thing was that the Robinsons had four girls who were part of the gang and we often played in their garden. On these occasions, Mr Robinson didn't mind in the least if we took an apple or two, but if he caught us scrumping them from the other side of the hedge he went crazy. It didn't stop us of course, and somehow, the illicit apples always tasted better.

Britain's birth rate shot up in the immediate post-war years so that, by the 1950s, the country was ankle deep in children. In the short street where I grew up there were nearly forty kids, all close enough in age to join in most of the games. For most fifties kids, their playground was either the street, any available piece of waste ground or bomb site, or, if you were lucky to have one, the local park. Playgrounds in the

fifties weren't the springy-surfaced, health and safety conscious places of today, far from it. Swings, slides and roundabouts were usually set into concrete or tarmac, and if you fell off it hurt, believe me! But that didn't stop us from swinging as high as we could and jumping off did it? Especially if we were double dared!

The Rag and Bone Man

It took a lot to distract us from our games, but some events were just too much resist and the arrival of the rag and bone man was one of those events. The rag and bone man and his horse and cart was a familiar sight on the streets of 1950s Britain. As kids, when we heard his cry, "*any old raaags,*" all games came to an abrupt halt, as we all ran into the house to hunt for unwanted items we could exchange for a balloon, or a goldfish in a bag filled with water.

These treasured prizes were obviously a bribe by the rag and bone man to get the neighbourhood kids to help fill his cart - and it worked a treat. It wasn't unheard of to see an angry mum chasing the rag and bone man down the street to recover her best blouse or dad's shirt.

Another interruption to my playtime was nowhere near as welcome as the rag and bone man.

To a young boy, playing and eating come very high in importance on the to do list. What doesn't is visiting grandma on a Sunday afternoon. Every Sunday afternoon without fail, I got the call from my mum to come in and get ready to go to my nan's. Don't get me wrong, I loved my nan dearly, but when visiting her interrupted an exciting game of hopscotch, or a crucial football match, the affection was severely tested. To make matters worse, I was made to dress in an outfit that could only have been designed by a sadist. It was a checked suit made of the itchiest material you can imagine. Furthermore, it had short trousers with a hem of the horrible cloth on the inside, which, despite my attempts to walk straight legged to stop it rubbing, drove me bonkers. The suit was the final straw that brought on a serious sulk, and to cap it all, to get to the bus stop, I had to walk past my stupid mates who were still playing their ridiculous games. They wouldn't say anything mean in front of my mum but I knew that inwardly they were mocking me. To be fair to my nan, I think she recognised my suffering and tried to ease it with slices of cottage loaf slathered with butter. It was some consolation I must admit.

Our Favourite Comics

A highlight of the childhood week was the day our favourite comic came out.

We couldn't wait to get our hands on the latest edition and were soon engrossed in the latest exploits of Desperate Dan, Dennis the Menace, and the Bash Street Kids. The most widely read comics in Britain in the 1950s were The Beano and The Dandy. More than two million of us read one or the other, or both, every week. The most popular reads for older boys were the Eagle and the Tiger with its hero, Roy of the Rovers. Roy Race of Melchester Rovers became so famous he got a whole comic to himself. Real Roy of the Rovers stuff that!

Older girls had their own favourites. Girl and School Friend, popular in the early fifties, were followed by Bunty, avidly read every week by hundreds of thousands of girls. Were you a member of the Bunty Club and do you remember the Four Mary's? The story of four girls at St Elmo's school ran for the whole life of the comic until its end in 2001. There was also Moira Kent, an aspiring ballerina, and the comic's namesake, Bunty, who, as I'm sure you know, was 'A Girl Like You.'

1951

May 3, 1951

As the King's words . . . 'I declare the Festival of Britain open' . . . roll around the world, in his Festival broadcast from the Steps of St Paul's Cathedral this morning, the Cathedral bells will peal out and then the bells of Britain from south to north, from east to west, will join in the Festival call. And this evening, on a blitzed site in the shadow of St Paul's, the youth of London – 5,000 of them – will light a giant bonfire that, like a Festival beacon, will spread the news again throughout the country. For more than 1,000 bonfires, organised by Britain's youth, will be lit this evening in all parts of the British Isles, and round these campfires will be sung the 'Song of the Festival,' written specially by Mr Harold Purcell.

June 21, 1951

The Government has again rejected a plea by the staff side of the Civil Service for equal pay for women.

The reason for rejecting the demand was that it would have far-reaching consequences, being a signal to industry and the rest of the community to make equal demands.

June 21, 1951

Belgian security officials are almost certain that Guy Burgess and Donald Maclean, the two missing British diplomats, sailed from Antwerp aboard a Soviet steamer either on June 1 or June 8.

One of the officials said that the men must have left the country with the help of a member of the Russian crew.

Revolting Youths

****

The Teenager is Born

In the mid-1950s, a revolution was gathering pace in Britain, one that would change the cultural landscape of the country forever and pave the way for 'the Swinging 60s'.

Until now young people had simply gone from childhood to adulthood with nothing in between. They wore the same style of clothes as their parents, had the same hair styles, and even listened to the same music, but change was in the air. By the mid-fifties the austerity of the war years was fading, unemployment was low, and a young person could leave school at 15 and easily find a job. Those who fancied a change could walk away from one position and quickly into another, often on the same day.

Wages, even for unskilled, work, were relatively high and many teenagers could make a reasonable contribution to the household budget and still have money to spare.

Big business was quick to recognise the spending power of teenagers, and shops began to promote fashions specially aimed at this new group of consumers.

Music also began to cater for the tastes of teenagers who were drawn to the more raunchy stuff coming out of America; Vera Lynn just didn't cut it any more.

But this trend didn't sit well with the old order according to this article from a Hertfordshire newspaper.

The world-famous Count Basie Band is dropped from a radio show because teenage listeners complain that it has a wrong beat. What in heavens name is music coming to?
Right now, Basie has one of the swingiest units in the world yet here are these musical morons claiming that the band has a wrong beat and causing its displacement. I suppose these self-same critics are the same people who call Elvis Presley musical!

Not a happy bunny then, but there was no stopping the march of the British teenagers. They were empowered, they had the money, they had the time, they had the fashion and music industries clambering to feed their desires, and nothing was going to stop them from having the time of their lives.

A lot of that time was spent in milk bars, which might not sound very radical today, but in the 1950s, the milk bar was the place to be. Here, over a milkshake or an ice cream, you could hang out with your friends, show off your new outfit, discuss which boys or girls you fancied, and listen to Bill Haley, Buddy Holly, or Elvis Presley blasting from the jukebox – in the right beat, obviously. Hanging out in the milk bar was innocent enough and just about acceptable to most parents, but there was another aspect of the teenage revolution the older generation found more difficult to accept.

Teddy Boys

Teddy Boys were a uniquely British phenomenon and first emerged in working-class areas of London in the early 1950s. They were defined, first and foremost, by their distinctive look. A long drape jacket, often with a velvet collar, a Slim Jim tie, narrow, high waisted 'drainpipe' trousers, and chunky crepe soled shoes, known as beetle-crushers or brothel-creepers. The hairstyle was also crucial. It could be a Tony Curtis, with a curled quiff and a crew cut on top, or a DA, short for Duck's Arse, with a large quiff at the front and the sides slicked back to form the shape of the rear end of a duck. These hairstyles required copious amounts of Brylcreem to keep them in place and the extravagant Teddy Boy look didn't come cheap. The whole outfit could cost as much as 5 weeks wages.

Because their clothes resembled those worn by dandies in the Edwardian era they were originally known as Edwardians. That changed in 1953 when an article in the Daily Express shortened it to 'Teddys' and the name stuck.

The Teds might have adopted the style of an earlier era, but it was the modern sound of the likes of Bill Haley and Elvis that provided the soundtrack for their youth rebellion. Sometimes though, the teenage uprising took on a more troubling nature.

When the film Rock Around The Clock came to the UK in 1956, Teddy Boys danced and sang in cinema aisles, tore up and slashed seats and generally caused mayhem.

Scenes like this had never been seen in Britain before, and the country suddenly woke up in shock to the subversive nature of the teenager. Panic swept through the establishment at what it described as the 'feral youth' and the 'teen menace'.

But there was worse to come. Some Teds formed gangs and gained notoriety following violent clashes with rival gangs, as well as unprovoked attacks on immigrants. The most notable clashes were the 1958 Notting Hill race riots.

According to one report;

"Teddy boys armed with iron bars, butcher's knives and weighted leather belts participated in mobs, 300- to 400-strong, that targeted black residents, leaving five black men lying unconscious on the pavements of Notting Hill."

The impression was that all Teddy Boys were violent thugs, which of course was far from the truth, as this recollection of one 50s Teddy Boy reveals.

"I had my first Ted suit in 1955 when I was 16 and ordered it unbeknown to my Mum & Dad because to them, Teddy Boys were taboo. When I wore the suit, I had to sneak out of the house without them seeing."

So much for the teenage rebel eh!

Whether they were hanging out in the milk bar, fighting in the street, or hiding their outfit from Mum & Dad, there was one aspect of teenage life in the 1950s that concerned all young men.

National Service

The National Service Act of 1948 made it compulsory for all healthy males between the ages of 17 and 21 to serve in the armed forces for 18 months.
In October 1950, in response to Britain's involvement in the war in Korea, the period was increased to 2 years.
The talk amongst youngsters was of resentment to this disruption to their lives, and their income.
Basic pay for a private soldier was around 30 shillings a week compared to £9 in Civvie Street and, while some went willingly, most were reluctant, although resigned to their fate.

Newspaper reports of British soldiers killed, wounded, or taken prisoner in Korea only heightened the concerns. When the official letter arrived instructing them to register for National Service, failing the medical seemed their only hope.

A few weeks after the indignity of dropping their trousers and coughing for the nurse, those deemed healthy enough received the dreaded plain, brown envelope. This was the instruction to report for basic training, which, for reasons no one seems to know, always started on a Thursday.

All new conscripts underwent six weeks of training designed to get them used to military life. There were endless drills, polishing kit for gruelling inspections, physical training, rifle practice, cross country runs, all to the soundtrack of corporals and sergeants shouting and swearing from morning till night.

NATIONAL SERVICE ACTS, 1948 TO 1955

**NOTICE TO MEN BORN BETWEEN
1st JULY, 1938, and 30th SEPTEMBER, 1938**

Requirement to Register at Local Offices of the Ministry of
Labour and National Service on Saturday, 17th November, 1956

In pursuance of the above Acts and of the Regulations made thereunder, all male British subjects within Great Britain who
were born between 1st July, 1938, and 30th September, 1938, both dates inclusive (with certain exceptions mentioned
below) are required to attend without fail for registration at a Local Office of the Ministry of Labour and National Service on

SATURDAY, 17th NOVEMBER, 1956

However, these hardships were the least of their worries.
When their training was completed, many raw recruits
were thrown into combat situations in places like Korea,
Malaya and Suez. Until the day their troopship pulled
into the port of these war torn regions, many of the
young soldiers had never before ventured further than
the streets of their home towns.

In a few weeks, carefree lives had been transformed and
the possibility of death or injury was a daily concern.
Around 200 conscripts were killed and many hundreds
more injured in Korea alone.

Despite these sad losses and the disruption to many
young lives, it must be said that some relished the opportunities National Service presented. It was a chance
to see parts of the world they could otherwise only have
dreamed of and some of the friendships formed during
National Service would last a lifetime.

The Korean War ended in 1953, but instead of celebrating, the conscripts, along with the majority of the British
public, watched in horror as its legacy unfolded.

The Cold War
****

Former allies in defeating Nazi Germany - the Soviet Union and America - took opposite sides during in the Korean War. The Soviets supported North Korea and the USA, South Korea. After the war ended the two super-powers, never exactly bosom buddies, turned on each other.

For those Britons who had lived through the dark days of the Second World War, it was with horror and disbelief that a new world conflict began to unfold. One that threatened death and destruction on an even greater scale. Britain sided with America and was quickly sucked in to what became known as the Cold War.

This war would be fought with weapons more terrible than any that had gone before.

The British people were already familiar with the awe-some power of nuclear weapons, having seen the news-reel footage and read the newspaper reports of the bombing of Hiroshima and Nagasaki in 1945.

The two bombs killed as many as 200,000 people and ended Japanese resistance in World War 2.

Reports of even more powerful weapons being tested by the USA in 1952, and the Soviet Union in 1953 were enough to send a shiver down the spine.

Britain joined the arms race in 1957 when it became the third nuclear power. At home, newspapers were full of stories of the devastation a nuclear attack would wreak. There was a concerted campaign to recruit civil defence volunteers, and civil defence exercises took place across the country.

By now, the Soviet President, Krushchev, was openly threatening the west with nuclear annihilation, boasting that Soviet missiles were capable of wiping out any American or European City. And if that wasn't enough, the information leaflets issued by the Government were clearly designed to scare the living daylights out of us.

(An example is produced on the next two pages.)

The threat of nuclear war was very real and truly terri-fying, and it was a cloud that would hang over the world for decades to come.

6 WHAT TO DO IMMEDIATELY AFTER ATTACK

FIRES

As soon as the blast wave has passed, go round the house and *put out any fires before they take hold.* Turn off the gas and any fuel oil supply, if that has not been done already. Try to make sure that you are safe from any fires which have started nearby.

WATER

If the mains supply is still functioning, you could use the water for fire-fighting. But as soon as possible *turn off the water supply at the stopcock to prevent the possibility of fall-out contaminated water entering the system.*

Remember that when the stopcock has been turned off, water heaters and boilers should also be turned off, or put out. To leave them going might be dangerous.

Tie up the ball-cock in the W.C. cistern, so that clean water is not used for flushing.

STOPCOCK

WATER HEATER

BOILER

These jobs are so important that they should be done despite the unknown risk from fall-out, but if you have to go outside put on gum-boots or stout shoes, a hat or headscarf, coat done up to the neck, and gloves. When you return, take these clothes off and leave them outside the fall-out room in case there is fall-out dust on them.

When you have seen to your own household, help any neighbour in need.

LISTEN FOR WARNING SIGNALS OF APPROACHING FALL-OUT

20

50

7 LIFE UNDER FALL-OUT CONDITIONS

THE FIRST DAYS

Once you know that there is danger from fall-out, **TAKE COVER AND DO NOT GO OUTSIDE AGAIN UNTIL YOU ARE TOLD BY WARDENS OR THE POLICE THAT IT IS SAFE TO DO SO.**

Listen for announcements on your radio. It will probably be safe to leave the fall-out room for short periods if visits to other parts of the house are necessary, for example, to obtain further supplies of food or water. *But do not go outside the house.*

This is only a general guide. The amount of fall-out would vary. It would be worst in the middle of the fall-out area, and would grow less and less towards the fringes. Everywhere, the danger from fall-out would grow less with time (see page 6).

You could not tell for yourself how bad fall-out was. This could be done only by people with special instruments, such as members of the civil defence, police and fire services. They would tell you when it was safe for you to come out in the open.

21

IN THE NEWS

1952

February 6, 1952

The King is Dead

The nation and Empire were stunned by the official announcement which came from Sandringham, at 10.45 a.m. today, that King George the Sixth, who retired to rest last night in his usual health, passed peacefully away in his sleep this morning. The King was in his 57th year, and the 16th of his reign.

February 7, 1952

Long Live the Queen

Queen Elizabeth the Second will be formally proclaimed Queen at St James Palace at 11 o'clock tomorrow morning. The arrangements are provisional, for they must be confirmed by the Queen who was flying through the night from Africa.

Goodbye to the Trams

July 6, 1952

Thousands of Londoners, some in paper hats, all of them in high spirits, and all, it seemed, determined to make the passing of the last tram a great occasion, lined the old steel road through South London, arms linked, as the very last tram of all screeched its way to the scrapyard at midnight last night.

Tea Galore

October 3, 1952

After twelve years the British cup of tea is set free. It was in July 1946 that our tea ration was set at a meagre two ounces a week. Now, from Sunday, tea coupons retreat into the past, and we can drink as much of our nation's favourite beverage as we like.

Home Life
****

Housing

At the dawn of the 1950s Britain was in the grip of a housing crisis. Wartime bombing and the programme of demolishing urban slums had created a serious shortage of homes.

It was common in those days for newly married couples to take a room in the house of in-laws, my own parents among them. They lived in my father's parent's 1930s semi-detached council house, along with my dad's brother, his wife, and their young son. The overcrowding increased when baby me joined the extended family, but we were lucky compared to the situation many families found themselves in. Slums still blighted many large towns and cities across the country and nearly half the population lived in low quality private rented accommodation.

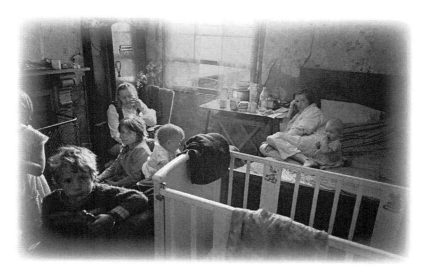

One account from Liverpool describes whole families living and sleeping in one room with nine dwellings sharing one lavatory in the yard and a two-ring stove on the landing. Water was supplied by one outside cold water tap for each dwelling, and public washhouses were the only way for many to wash their clothes and themselves properly.

More comfortable were the two up, two down Victorian terraced houses that were a feature of most towns and cities. They were more spacious with two bedrooms upstairs and a kitchen and parlour downstairs. Even so, in larger

families, several children often shared a bed.

Goin' out the back.

Although these houses usually had the luxury of their own lavatory instead of sharing, it was still outside in the back yard in a small brick or wooden building. "Goin' out the back" was a common euphemism for going to the loo, and, "don't forget to pull the chain," was often the response. The chain hung from the water tank above the toilet and required a tug to flush it. Using the outdoor loo was bearable in the warmer months but imagine trudging down the yard in the dark in sub-zero temperatures to do your business. Not surprisingly, when winter set in, chamber pots were removed from closets, dusted off, and put to good use.

Toilet paper was usually torn up newspapers on a piece of string, not ideal by any means, but infinitely preferable to that rough, transparent, medicated stuff, the dreaded Izal.

Mother does know best...

There is always one thing of real importance to consider—the health of the family. That is why mother chooses the Izal Toilet Roll. She knows that each smooth sheet is medicated with Izal Germicide, and that a fine strong tissue is an hygienic necessity.

IZAL
MEDICATED TOILET ROLL

Give me a Daily Sketch any day!

Mind you, Izal did make decent tracing paper, and also a pretty good kazoo when it was wrapped around a comb.

The solution to the housing shortage was obviously to build more homes and more than two million of them went up during the 1950s, two thirds of them local authority housing, many in large new council estates.

BARROW BROS.

(BUILDERS, LANCASTER) LTD.

HOUSES
FOR SALE

NEWLANDS ESTATE,
BOWERHAM

3 Bedrooms — £2,050
(now available)

2 Bedrooms — £1,830

90% MORTGAGE OVER 25 YEARS AT 4%
NO ROAD CHARGES.

APPLY

BULK ROAD, LANCASTER

For the lucky few that could afford it, the 1950s provided more opportunities to buy your own house. In 1952 the average cost of a house was £1891, equivalent to £38,800 today. This was around 4 times the average salary compared to more than 8 times in today's market.

For those who lived in newer homes, the uncomfortable process of 'goin out the back' was replaced by an altogether more pleasant visit to 'the smallest room in the house'. However, some older folk thought doing your business inside the house was downright disgusting.

Coal Fires

What most 1950s homes had in common, old and new, was the absence of central heating and, in the wintertime, our houses were very chilly places indeed.

I remember going to bed fully clothed and wriggling around to generate some friction, removing layers of clothing as the bed warmed up.

In the morning, in the depths of winter, it was quite common to wake up with ice on the inside of the bedroom windows. It might sound like a cliché, but, believe me, it's absolutely true.

Quite often the only source of heat was a coal fire in the main living room of the house or, in old houses, the range in the kitchen.

In the colder months, regular deliveries by the coal man were vital in maintaining the little warmth we could squeeze from our draughty dwellings. He arrived in his lorry, or sometimes a horse-drawn wagon, laden with hundred-weight sacks of coal. To children the coal man was a fascinating, slightly scary figure, black as the ace of spades from the coal dust, apart from pale rings around his eyes where he'd rubbed the dust away.

The coal man swung the sack, seemingly effortlessly,
onto his back and emptied it into wherever the coal was
stored - the coal-house or bunker, or, in some Victorian
terraced properties, via a coal hole into a cellar underneath the house.

Does anyone remember searching in the coal house for
fossils in the coal?

The painstaking process of building a fire was so commonplace it was a widely held skill, and the job often fell
to the oldest child.

Screwed up pieces of newspaper that would burn easily
made up the first layer in the empty grate. Next were
small dry twigs or wood shavings for kindling.

Finally, some carefully selected small lumps of coal transferred from the coal house to the fireplace with the use of a scuttle, and then the exciting bit – setting fire to the precisely constructed creation.

But it didn't always work out did it?

If the wind was in the wrong direction, or if it was too strong or not strong enough, the fire didn't take. Then it was time for the experts to take over to 'draw' the fire.

This meant holding something like a sheet of newspaper across the front of the fireplace to direct the airflow up the chimney, and at the same time keeping a close eye on the newspaper. If it started to turn brown, it had to be removed immediately before it caught fire.

What on earth would we have done without newspapers?

After an agonizing wait, if all went well, we would hear the glorious sound of a fire roaring away behind the newspaper, and all was well with the world.

The fire might still need some encouragement now and again and there was always a poker on hand to rearrange the burning coals or break them up to let in more air. There was something immensely satisfying about getting a fire going, something primeval we shared with our stone age ancestors that we just don't get from turning up the central heating. There were also plenty of things that could go wrong.

There was the ever-present risk of a chimney fire, which, if it couldn't be extinguished quickly, resulted in a visit by the fire brigade. Great excitement for the neighbours, but oh! the shame of it.

The best way to avoid a chimney fire was to have it swept regularly, but what a palaver that was.

The day before the sweeps' visit, all furniture in the room was either removed or covered, and ornaments, pictures, and anything else that could be contaminated by the cloud of soot that was soon to fill the room was put away.

The sweep arrived with his intriguing array of rods, brushes, sacks, and cloths and set about his task. After a while he shouted 'out' and whoever had been assigned the important job of waiting outside for the brush to appear from the top of the chimney responded with 'out' in confirmation.

The sweep then pulled the brush back down bringing with it a heap of soot and a cloud of dust that filled the room and coated every surface in it.

The sweep was only an occasional nuisance, but coal fires were messy things each and every day.

Before the ritual lighting of the fire could begin again, the previous day's ashes had to be cleared from the grate, which involved carrying them through the house to the dustbin. Did you know they're called dustbins because that's where we put the ashes from the fire? I didn't!

In some houses the coal fire served a purpose other than keeping us warm. Some had a boiler behind the fire for heating water. A pull-out damper directed hot gases from the fire onto the back boiler to heat water for the household. I know we take it completely for granted today but back then, hot water on tap was a rare luxury and one of the few wintertime perks.

As they say though, 'no gain without pain', and on one occasion in my household, the pain was rather acute.

I got home from school one winter's afternoon and was a little put out that my mother wasn't there with her usual cheery greeting. I then became aware of raised voices in the lounge and went to investigate. As I got closer, I gathered that my mum was distraught, and my dad was flustered and a little angry. When I poked my head round the door the cause of their distress was obvious. There was black water all over the normally spotless lounge floor and, around the fireplace, a layer of black sludge. It turned out the back boiler had burst, spilling its contents all over the floor and bringing with it as much soot as it could gather on the way.

I don't remember the clean-up but, judging by the mess I do remember, it must have taken a very long time indeed.

The End of Coal

Chimney fires, messy visits by the chimney sweep, and the occasional burst boiler were bad enough, but there was a far more deadly result of our widespread use of coal. In the colder months when the fires were burning, it was quite common for towns and cities to be enveloped by thick fog, or smog as it was known, a mixture of smoke and fog. As I recall, the fog was often particularly dense after Guy Fawkes Night when hundreds of bonfires added to the pollution.

As a child it was actually quite exciting to venture outside and be swallowed up by the thick grey blanket, unable to see more than a few feet in front of you.

These 'peasoupers' though, were a major hazard to our health and things came to a head in December 1952. In London, a period of unusually cold weather combined with near windless conditions caused a thick blanket of smog to settle.

It lasted for 5 days, brought traffic to a standstill, and even seeped into homes. Worst of all was the effect on people's health.

It's estimated that more than 4000 people died in the immediate aftermath of the 'Great Smog', with a further 8000 deaths from its effects in the following weeks.

It was obvious that air pollution was a killer, and the Great Smog lead ultimately to the Clean Air Act of 1956, which made the use of smokeless fuels mandatory. It would take a while, but eventually most built-up areas became smokeless zones.

As a child in the 1950s coal fires were a part of everyday life. Yes, they were messy, yes, they were smelly, and as we know now, they were extremely bad for us. While I'm obviously glad to see the back of them, particularly for my grand children's sake, I can't help thinking of them with a fond nostalgia. There was something immensely satisfying about an open fire, no doubt enhanced by the effort it took to get them going.

They also had some practical uses other than keeping us warm, especially at Christmas. I remember my dad lining chestnuts up on the front of the grate while I waited impatiently for them to split open. Finally ready to eat – they were delicious.

Try doing that with a radiator!

Of course, I've got used to life without coal fires but even now, if I venture into an area where open fires still burn, the unmistakable smell takes me right back to my childhood.

Bath Night

Forget a quick shower, forget a luxurious soak in the bath, in the 1950s, for most of us, bathing was something to be endured rather than enjoyed.

Today all that is required is a turn of a tap, a tug of a cord, or a flick of a switch and away we go, but in the fifties it was far from straightforward. It was no wonder many of us only took a bath once a week, whether we needed it or not!

Bath night was usually on a Sunday so that everyone was nice and clean for the start of the new week. For houses without a dedicated bathroom, the bath itself was a galvanised tin tub that was kept in the outside privy and brought out on bath night. It was filled with hot water, either from kettles and saucepans boiled on the stove, or from the wash copper and it was quite normal for the whole family to use same water. Father went in first and the kids followed, oldest first, down to the  youngest, all scrubbed with household soap and rinsed off using a jug. It was said that nobody ever got really clean until they left home.

IN THE NEWS
1953

February 1, 1953

Hurricane Horror

There were 177 people on board the steamer Princess Victoria as she drifted helplessly to destruction off the Irish Coast yesterday – 177 passengers, 54 crew – and for six hours they knew that they were drifting towards death.

Forty-eight, the lucky ones, survived: 139 died. But from the moment the steering broke down in the worst Atlantic storm for years, everybody aboard knew that their lives were in the balance.

June 3, 1953

The Queen Lights up London

Queen Elizabeth the Second, home from her crowning, stepped out on to the balcony of Buckingham Palace at 9.45 last night. She touched a switch and lights of Coronation London blazed out. The great crowd that had surged all evening round the Palace since the Queen rode home from the Abbey broke into fresh cheers.

June 3, 1953

The TV Coronation

In Ilmington and many of the surrounding villages the first signs of Coronation Day were to be found in the sight of families setting out from home carrying small cases or neat brown paper parcels.

Those cases and parcels contained sandwiches, and thus equipped, hundreds set out to spend the day with relatives or friends watching the pageantry of the Coronation on television. Indeed, it would be no exaggeration to call this the TV coronation.

June 3 1953

People started to queue outside the Embassy Ballroom in Skegness as early as 8 a.m. although the Coronation broadcast was not due to start until 10.15 a.m.

Meanwhile a TV set had been installed in the Assembly Hall, Alexandra Road by the Nottingham Cooperative Society and a crowd of nearly 400 pensioners, many of whom were seeing TV for the first time, had their own special Coronation show.

June 3, 1953

Party Time

The party for 47 children in Dace Road, Bethnal Green, was one of thousands happening all over Britain yesterday. The children enjoyed a banquet of sandwiches, jelly, and cakes, washed down with gallons of lemonade and each one was presented with a souvenir mug with their name engraved on it. You can be sure that, in the future, Dace Road will celebrate other great occasions with other parties. You can be sure too, that at them, people will be saying: 'Ah, but you should have seen the one we had on Coronation Day.'

June 15, 1953

Crowd Rush to See Execution Notice

Hundreds of people waited outside Pentonville Prison today for the notices announcing the execution of John Christie, the man who lived and murdered at 10, Rillington Place, Notting Hill. There was nothing of the usual sombre hush and even as Christie's moment of death passed the crowd continued gossiping, laughing, and joking. There are moves afoot for Timothy Evans to be pardoned. Evans was hanged for the murder of his baby daughter at 10 Rillington Place.

IN THE NEWS
1954

May 7, 1954

Wonderful Bannister!
The fabulous, fantastic, for-minute mile has been
achieved at last – by Britain's wonder runner,
Roger Bannister, twenty-four-year-old St Mary's
Hospital medical student. At Iffley Road, Oxford,
last night he shattered the world record with the
greatest performance in athletics history.

July 3, 1954

We Can Throw Away Those Ration Books
After today, meat, the last rationed commodity is
freed. All except children entitled to free milk can
tear up their ration books.
Farmers, butchers and slaughterhouse men are
working overtime to have a first-class display in
the shops on Monday.
Women intend to celebrate today with a rally in
Trafalgar Square

A 1950s Housewife
****

The lives of women in the 1950s were a world away from those of the independent, emancipated ladies of today, and fifties housewives were expected to conform to the rules society had laid down.

As we've seen, part of their education was geared to producing good housewives. Most women left school and went straight into work until they married, and were then expected to raise children and keep house.

A handful of women, around one in a hundred, did manage to avoid the inevitable and went to university, but they were very much the exception.

At the other end of the scale there were women who had homes and families to look after, but also had to work to make ends meet. For them, life was exceptionally hard and many were forced to take whatever menial tasks they could.

Cleaning for better off households, taking in washing or ironing, anything that would bring in a few shillings to put food on the table or keep a roof over their children's heads.

Most women were consigned to a life of domesticity and, without the mod-cons we're used to today, it was hard work to say the least. Take wash day for example.

Wash Day

In the early 1950s, few households had washing machines so doing the weekly wash was an exhausting process that took all day.

Needless to say, all reasonable efforts were made to keep washing to a minimum. One set of underwear, comprising a vest and pants for example, lasted all week, and was only changed on bath night.

In villages, towns, and cities, up and down the country, wash day was Monday, and it had been that way for as long as anyone could remember.

Various reasons have been suggested for this universal practice. Some say it was because the day's main meal could be made of leftovers from Sunday, therefore leaving more time to spend on the washing. Others claim that it was because factories were closed on Sundays so the air was cleaner on Monday; or was it because housewives could rest on Sunday and were better prepared for the physical demands of doing the washing. Whatever the reason, come Monday morning, the housewives of Britain became a formidable army of washerwomen, loading their gas fired wash coppers and wielding their wash dollies and copper sticks.

A wash copper was a metal boiler used for household washing and heated by coal or gas. They were originally made of copper, hence the name, although by the fifties most were made of galvanized iron.

Clothes inside the copper were agitated by hand using a washing dolly or a round wooden baton called a copper stick. When the copper wasn't being used for the weekly wash it was also useful for boiling puddings, and many a wonderful Christmas Pudding has emerged, steaming from the wash copper. Wash day was such a major event in most British households, it has left many people who grew up in the 1950s with lasting memories. I personally have a vivid recollection of the copper stick, which was an ever-present object throughout my childhood.

It was smooth and bleached white from use, and when it wasn't wash day, served all sorts of childish purposes. It doubled as a sword, a magic wand, a gun, and anything else my fertile imagination could conjure up.

When mum was satisfied the washing was clean, she removed it from the copper to start the painstaking process of drying. The first stage, and the most fascinating in my opinion, was putting it through the mangle.

This was a fearsome looking thing with two large rollers, metal cogs, and a metal handle that, when it was turned, forced the washing through the rollers to press out excess water.

Once the washing was well and truly mangled, it was time for the hanging out ceremony, outside if it was fine, and it was uncanny how all the ladies in the street began this part of the task at the same time.

Before long there were endless rows of washing flapping in the breeze, held in place on the line by wooden pegs and held up by the clothes prop, and anyone who lit a bonfire on wash day risked the wrath of the washer-women's army.

As the 1950s progressed technology began to make life easier for the hard-pressed housewife, at least those who could afford it, more to the point, whose husbands could. It was a sign of the times that the adverts for these gadgets were aimed at men. After all, a mere woman couldn't possibly make such an important decision.

Wash day was hard work and a break for a chat over the fence was well-earned.

It's Never Done!

Another opportunity to catch up on the neighbourhood gossip was the weekly task of scrubbing the front step. It seems a very odd thing to do now but in the 1950s, a spotlessly clean step was a matter of pride, no matter how ramshackle the house was.

Some conscientious housewives even extended the chore to include sweeping and washing the patch of pavement outside the house.

Other regular tasks a lot of modern women wouldn't even contemplate are sewing, darning, and knitting, but in the 1950s these were essential skills, and you were just as likely to see a Singer sewing machine sitting in the corner of the room as a television set.

If a sock had a whole in it, you darned it; if little Johnny split his blazer you sewed it, and it was common to see children out and about wearing, dresses, cardies, and jumpers made by their mothers.

My mother was an avid knitter, and her knitting basket with its balls of coloured wool, different sized needles, and complex patterns, a held a certain allure for an inquisitive young boy.

She would sit for hours each evening, knitting needles clacking away rapidly, and glancing occasionally at the pattern as a new garment grew before my very eyes.

(As I'm writing this I'm thinking 'knit one, pearl one' and I don't know why.)

The extraordinary thing was that she could hold a conversation while she was performing the complicated process.

Sometimes though, things went wrong.

I remember one time she had knitted a jumper for my dad, but when he tried it on, it reached down almost to his knees and the sleeves were about six inches too long.

It became a standing family joke and whenever my dad wanted to wind up my mum, he would don his oversized jumper.

Feeding the Family

Feeding the family was another exercise in planning, per-
severance, and fortitude for the 1950s housewife.
In the early fifties, only the wealthiest households had
a fridge (the nearest most of us got was a pantry with a
cold shelf) so shopping for food was an essential part of
the housewife's daily routine. In most older neighbourhoods there was a corner shop, an 'Open all Hours' type
of place, where you could pick up a few essentials if you
ran out. In older neighbourhoods these were usually a
former house with the old front room turned
into the actual shop. On
our new estate, the equivalent of the corner shop
was a wooden shack,
where Mr Ravenhill sold
a range of non perishable
goods, like tinned food,
cigarettes, sweets out of
jars, and an item I remember clearly, liquorice root.
This was basically a stick
that tasted of liquorice and
you could chew for hours.

It was sold as a sweet and during rationing was often one
of the few things available. You can still get liquorice
root but now it's sold in health shops. I wonder if that
will happen to chocolate - we can but hope!

Our main shopping was done at the 'Big Shops' about twenty minutes walk away
There was a baker, a butcher, a grocer and a green grocer and most of them were family businesses. They knew their customers by name and were happy to stop for a chat, which seems to have been an essential part of 1950s life.

To make the housewives life a little easier, some of the shopkeepers offered a home delivery service (there's a novel idea). This was usually carried out by a boy on a bike with a basket on the front.
The stuff we bought was different too.
The tea bag was a long way off yet and tea was sold loose in a bag; ham and cheese were sliced before your eyes; bread was freshly baked and wrapped in a sheet of tissue. This could be used later as toilet paper - a rare bit of fifties loo luxury.

At the greengrocers, fruit and vegetables were loose and sold in paper bags, and because virtually nothing was imported, they were all seasonal. Strawberries for example were grown locally and were only available for a short time each year - and didn't they taste better for it!

Food, like many things in fifties, was hard work, and when we got our shopping home, peas had to be shelled, potatoes and carrots washed, and poultry cleaned out and stuffed.

To make things even more difficult, in the first part of the fifties, a variety of staple foods like sugar, butter, cheese, margarine, bacon, meat and tea were still rationed. Everyone in the family needed a Ministry of Food ration book, which entitled the holder

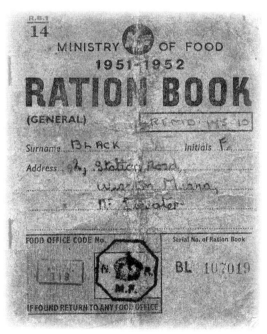

to their weekly helping of whatever happened to be available, and it was rarely enough to feed the family. There was widespread relief in July 1954 when 14 years of food rationing finally ended.

IN THE NEWS
1955

July 13, 1955

Protest Scenes as Ruth Ellis Hangs

Some women wept and others prayed as Ruth Ellis, 28-year-old mother of two children, was hanged at Holloway Prison today for the murder of the man who had been her lover.

Mrs Ellis had been sentenced for the murder of 25 year-old David Blakely, a racing motorist with whom she had been living. She shot him outside a public house.

Ruth Ellis was the 15th woman to be hanged for murder in Britain this century.

September 5, 1955

No Supper on Sunday

For years Mr and Mrs Veal have been serving fish and chips on summer Sunday night to motorists on their way home from Blackpool. Then a police sergeant and constable called. The Veals were told that their shop is 200 yards outside the law. That is how far they are outside the Blackpool boundary where fish and chip shops are allowed to stay open on Sunday Nights.

Food in the Fifties
****

The range of things we eat has increased dramatically since the 1950s. Back then McDonald's came from Scotland, Curry was the surname of one of my schoolteachers; pizza was something to do with a wonky tower in Italy; rice was just a pudding; the only frozen food was ice cream; and we'd never heard of yoghurt.

Even the names of our mealtimes have changed. Dinnertime was in the middle of the day, the evening meal was at teatime, and lunch, what on earth was that? The only mealtime that hasn't changed since the fifties is breakfast, and a lot of the things we eat for breakfast today were familiar back then.

Quaker introduced Sugar Puffs in 1955 using a steam train in their advertising. The Sugar Puff bear appeared in 1956, joining Snap, Crackle and Pop in promoting their cereals to children. There were also plastic cars, rockets, and other miniature inducements inside the packs to make us nag mum to buy the cereal with the best toys.

Many fifties kids, me included, will remember searching among the cereal for the little toy when mum wasn't looking.

The staple diet for most families in the 1950s was meat and two veg, in various forms, which, compared with today's spicey offerings, sounds rather bland. This was more than made up for though, by our glorious puddings. Jam Roly-Poly, Apple Pie, Spotted Dick, Bread and Butter Pudding, were all helped down with a generous covering of custard.

If money was short or time was tight, a banana filled the gap, with a dollop of custard obviously, and a rice pudding with skin on the top always went down well. I also remember my mother serving up tinned peaches and bread and butter, which, with hindsight, seems a peculiar combination – but it was delicious! If we fancied a snack between meals, which was pretty much always, the go to option was bread and dripping, perfect with a sprinkling of salt.

'Fast' Food

In the fifties, a fast-food delivery meant dad going to the fish and chip shop on his bike. It seemed to take ages and mum reckoned he stopped off at the pub on the way. When the food finally arrived, the mouthwatering smell permeating yesterday's newspaper was worth the wait. Another rare treat when I was young was going to the chippy with my mates for 'sixpenneth of chips' to share. If we asked nicely, and the chippy was in a good mood, we might even get a free helping of scraps, those little bits of batter from the bottom of the fish fryer.

Eating Out

For many people in the 1950s, eating out was a rarity. The nearest most came was a visit to the local cafe or a bag of cockles, whelks or jellied eels from the seafood man.

For a very special occasion, and if we could afford it, we might stretch to a trip to a Lyons tea shop for a cuppa and a piece of cake, although that meant putting on our

Sunday best. A treat for the youngsters was a bottle of pop (my kids laugh when I call it pop) and a bag of crisps, one flavour only, plain, with a little blue bag of salt inside the packet. Things started to change when the UK's answer to the burger bars in America arrived in the 1950s to cater for the teenagers. The first Wimpy Bar opened in 1954 selling hamburgers and milk-shakes and quickly proved popular with young people.

Two years later, another iconic eatery made its debut when the first Berni Inn opened in Bristol. Before long the country was awash with Wimpy Bars and Berni Inns and the idea of eating out was growing on us.

Those with more exotic tastes also had options as more and more Chinese restaurants appeared in the late fifties. Never one to miss an opportunity, in 1958, Billy Butlin introduced chop suey and chips into his holiday camps.

Home Entertainment
****

The Radio

In the 1950s, certainly in the early years of the decade, the majority of people relied on their radio for their home entertainment. In the mornings, the BBC Light Programme broadcast shows for the busy housewife, classics like Listen While You Work and Mrs Dale's Diary.

On the 16th of January 1950 the BBC launched Listen With Mother. It was aimed at the under 5's and broadcast after youngsters had eaten their dinner and could concentrate properly, and mother, hopefully, had time to sit with them. The phrase "Are you sitting comfortably? Then I'll begin", became part of British folklore.

Later in the day, at 5 o'clock, it was time for Children's Hour, which was aimed at older children home from school.

Popular series on children's hour you might remember were, Out with Romany, Sherlock Holmes, Toytown, and Worzel Gummidge. We all had our own favourites and there were plenty to choose from, but for generations of children, the highlight of the week was on Saturday morning.

Children's Favourites, hosted by Uncle Mac, began at 9 o'clock with the opening words "Hello children every-where" followed by the theme tune, 'Puffin Billy'. The program was unique in that children wrote in with song requests and each week, a few lucky ones had their names read out, guaranteeing a brief spell of fame at school on Monday. Then there were the songs, – Nellie the Elephant, I Tawt I Saw a Puddy Tat, The Kings New Clothes, The Hippopotamus Song, and who could forget Arthur Askey's Bee Song - absolute classics.

New Year's Day 1951 saw the start of a broadcasting phenomenon with the airing of the very first episode of the Archers.

Dan Archer had the opening line, "And a Happy New Year to all," and this everyday story of country folk is now the longest running drama in the world.

By 1953 it was attracting nine million listeners, my mother among them, so I grew up with the Archers.

I remember listening to the evening broadcast (I think it was around 7 o'clock) with my mother. As soon as it finished it was bedtime and, all these years later, if I hear the old Archers theme tune, I could quite happily go to bed.

Sunday was a big day on the wireless, after all, on a wet winter's day in the fifties, there wasn't much else to do. The Billy Cotton Band Show kicked things off, starting with an over the-top, and very loud, "Wakey Wake-aaay" from the big man himself. The Band Show was followed by a comedy series, classics like The Navy Lark, Life with the Lyons, and Hancock's Half Hour.

Those who wanted something a little more radical could tune into a new comedy series called Crazy People, written by a relative unknown called Spike Milligan.
It premiered in 1951 with a modest audience of 370,000. By the end of the 17th show it was pulling in nearly 2 million and had been renamed the Goon Show. Neddie Seagoon, Eccles, and Bluebottle, alias Harry Secombe, Spike Milligan, and Peter Sellers, were set to become household names.

The Gramaphone

The 1950s saw the growing popularity of another form of home entertainment – the gramaphone.
More and more British households were acquiring the machines that allowed them to play their favourite music whenever they wanted. Some people even had a radiogram, which combined the radio and gramaphone in one unit, often cleverly disguised as a sideboard.

They looked conventional enough, but these apparently innocent pieces of furniture played their part in a cultural revolution. Our choice of listening was no longer controlled by the BBC, and it wasn't always what the authorities would have picked for us.

In 1955, the best selling record was Rock Around the Clock by Bill Haley and the Comets. It was loud, it was brash, and some said subversive, but it was so much fun.

The Television Age

For anyone who has grown up with 24 hour, streaming, catch up, on demand TV on countless channels, it's impossible to imagine life without television, but in 1950 less than one in ten households had a TV set.

Everything changed in 1953. When it was announced that the BBC was to show the Coronation of Queen Elizabeth II live on television on the 2nd of June, it caused a rush to get one of those new-fangled TV sets.

Newspapers were full of adverts urging us to buy or rent our sets in time for the big day, and it worked.

The number of homes with a TV set more than doubled in the run up to the Coronation, despite the cost. The price of the cheapest 12 inch set was equivalent to almost £1800 today. Even to rent a set cost around £20 a week at today's prices.

Many of those who hadn't managed to get a TV were invited into the homes of friends and neighbours to watch the coronation.

The Chance of a Life-Time is Yours

LET US PROVIDE THAT CHANCE BY TELEVISION. STILL TIME TO GET YOUR TELEVISION INSTALLED BEFORE

CORONATION

In stock at time of going to press

His Master's Voice 15in. Console	119 gns.
Ultra 15in. Console	£99 13 0
Ultra 12in. Console	85 gns.
Philips 12in. Console	£88 2 11
Philips 12in. Console	£78 9 2
Bush 16in. Console	115 gns.
Bush 14in. Console	85 gns.
Bush 12in. Table Model	60 gns.
Ekco 12in. Console	£78 0 0
G.E.C. 12in. Table Model	57 gns.
G.E.C. 12in. Console	71 gns.
Ultra 12in. Table Model	61½ gns.
Ekco 15in. Table Model	£86 0 0
R.G.D. 12in. Console	91 gns.
R.G.D. 12in. Table Model	67 gns.

AND MANY OTHERS

Also we offer you in Refrigerators

Astral Table Model	£45 13 11
Wallis Floor Model	£54 12 0
Coldstor Floor Model	£82

MORPHY RICHARDS. These famous Irons can now be purchased at small monthly payments.

THE STORE IS

H. GALE

TOWN HALL, MARKET SQUARE, BIGGLESWADE, Beds.

Phone 3178

29 HIGH ST., SANDY, Beds.

Phone 170

At the start of the broadcast, commentator Richard Dimbleby, told the transfixed viewers; *"So today the Queen will ascend the steps of her throne in the sight of a great multitude of people."*
The television age had arrived, and life would never be quite the same.

By the end of the decade, nearly three quarters of the population had a TV, although in the 1950s, the viewing experience wasn't quite what we've come to expect. There was one BBC channel, black and white of course, and the hours we could watch were tightly controlled by the Postmaster General. The BBC could only broadcast between 9am and 11pm and no more than 2 hours of TV were allowed before 1pm.

Almost everyone of a certain age will remember Watch With Mother, the TV version of Listen With Mother. It was aimed at pre-school children and broadcast each day at 1.30.

A generation of children grew up with Andy Pandy, Rag, Tag and Bobtail, The Woodentops, and my own favourite, The Flower Pot Men – was it Bill or was it Ben? I think the little house knew something about it, don't you?

There was also a period between 6pm and 7pm when no programmes could be broadcast. This was known as 'the toddlers truce' and was used to trick young children into thinking TV had finished for the day and it was time for bed.

With the kids out of the way, the grown-ups could settle down to watch their own programmes, eager to catch up on the trials and tribulations of the Grove Family, Britain's very first TV soap opera.

Soon a posh BBC announcer wished all a very good night, the test card appeared, and the National Anthem made sure we knew that was our lot for the evening.

The BBC's monopoly came to an end in September 1955 with the launch of ITV London. With it came the birth of TV adverts; the first was for Gibbs SR toothpaste. But the BBC wouldn't surrender its position meekly.

On the day of ITV's launch it killed off one of the best loved characters in the Archers, Grace Archer, in a stable fire. The following day BBC's switchboard was jammed with distraught callers and the event stole the headlines in the newspapers, which of course, was exactly what the BBC intended.

But commercial television wasn't going away and by 1957 it had extended its reach to most of the country.

Do you remember this comic bunch in The Army Game? From left to right. Front row: Sgt. Maj. Snudge (Bill Fraser) Capt.T.R. Pocket (Frank Williams) Cpl. "Flogger" Hoskins (Harry Fowler) Back row: Pte. Montague "Excused Boots" Bisley (Alfie Bass) Pte. Leonard Bone (Ted Lune) L/Cpl. Ernest "Moosh" Merryweather (Mario Fabrizi)

Shows like The Army Game, The Arthur Haynes Show, and Emergency Ward 10 kept us entertained, and how on earth did we survive before TV ads told us what we should be buying. How would we have known otherwise we should, 'Go to work on an egg'; that Murray Mints were the 'too good to hurry mints'; or that the 'Esso sign means happy motoring'; and lord knows how many fruit gums mum would have forgotten.

IN THE NEWS
1956

March 6, 1956

Fame From Records

An example of that modern phenomenon, the 'pop singer' is on view at the Theatre Royal, Portsmouth, this week, in the person of Ronnie Hilton.

He has rocketed to the top of the bill as a result of his gramaphone records.

May 8, 1956

Not proven – this was the verdict on the relationship between smoking and lung cancer delivered by Mr Robin Turton, the Minister of Health, in the Commons today.

In view of the state of the evidence, Mr Turton very properly rejected the suggestion of a Socialist M.P. for a publicity campaign on the dangers of tobacco.

September 26, 1956

Superintendent Redfern asked for the maximum penalty on a youth accused at Derby today of riotous behaviour following a performance of the film "Rock Around the Clock".
Superintendent Redfern said: "Whether the police did right in bringing him to court or whether he should have gone to the mental health welfare officer I am not sure. He was singing and dancing on top of a telephone kiosk."

November 1, 1956

Thousands Queue To Buy First 'Lucky Dip' Bonds
National Savings Premium Bonds, with a chance of winning anything from £25 to £1000, are on sale today in 20,000 post offices and 13,000 branches of banks.
'Savings with a thrill' is the new slogan which launches the campaign.
There were big queues at some post offices from 8 a.m. and thousands of people bought their 'lucky dip' bonds on the way to work.

Going Out
****

Going to the Pictures

What we didn't do in the 1950s, hardly any of us anyway, was go to the cinema. We went to the pictures instead. Almost every community had its picture house, whether part of a chain like the ABC, Gaumont, Odeon and Savoy, or one of a host of independents.

Where I lived we had three cinemas. Our local was a 20 minute walk away, and two larger and grander ones were a short bus ride.

There were clear distinctions between small local neighbourhood cinemas, 'fleapits' as they were often known, and their posh town centre counterparts, distinctions that were reflected in the prices.

This description of a local fleapit might strike a cord with some readers.

"The manager arrived on a bike, went inside and switched the lights on, sold you a ticket, came round the other side and tore it in two, then ran down with a torch and showed to your seat – if he could be bothered."

At the larger cinemas, generally those belonging to a chain, the experience was considerably better. They were bigger, the decor was smarter, the seats were plusher, uniformed usherettes showed you to them, then walked up and down the aisles selling ice cream from trays in the interval. The seats in the main theatre were the stalls with the cheapest seats at the front because you had to crick your neck to look up at the screen. These were known as the one and nines, because, you've guessed it, they cost 1/-9d. The rear stalls were more costly because of the better viewing position. They were also popular with courting couples because they offered a bit more privacy.

Above the stalls was the circle, the most expensive place to sit. Even the toilets in the better cinemas provided a touch of luxury most people in the fifties didn't enjoy, even at home, such as hot and cold running water and large mirrors. Mind you, if my experience is anything to go by, the architects could have thought a little more about the location of the toilets. At our local ABC cinema they were accessed via a ramp at the front of the auditorium either side of the screen. If the audience wasn't particularly gripped by the film, your walk up the ramp was often accompanied by a chorus of, "we know where you're going,", and after you'd done the necessary, "we know where you've been."

All good natured, but very embarrassing.

There were usually two films, an A and B, plus Pathe News, and adverts for local businesses. It didn't matter what time you arrived, because you could stay until the part you'd missed came around again.

My first trip to the pictures is something I've never forgotten. My parents took me to see South Pacific in glorious technicolour. I was incredibly excited just to be in this extraordinary place, but as soon as the film started, I was totally transfixed. I haven't watched it again for many years but I'm sure I could sing along to 'Happy Talk' no problem.

Not long after this experience I was actually allowed to come to this fantastic place on Saturday mornings with just my mates, but more about that later.

For many people, cinemas in the 1950s were much more than somewhere to watch a film, they were an important part of their social life.

Cinema foyers were a meeting place for teenage boys and girls who hung around in groups and, it must be said, often indulged in horseplay, much to the irritation of the older clientele. Boys whistled at the girls or jeered at friends who were waiting for their first date.

If a boy was lucky enough to get a date, he would avoid the local fleapit and take the girl somewhere grander to impress. Mind you, the level of romance was usually dictated by the current financial situation. If things were tight, it was quite normal for the boy to suggest meeting inside, so he didn't have to pay for his date.

By now American influences were beginning to have an impact on British culture, particularly among young people, sometimes with disturbing consequences.

When the film Rock Around the clock was released in Britain in 1956, young people in cinemas across the country were reported as going 'wild in the aisles' dancing and even tearing up cinema seats.

Following this the film was banned from being shown by some cinemas for fear of further trouble.

The Sixpenny Crush

Just as lively, but far more innocent, were the Saturday children's matinees, the Sixpenny Crush as they were known.

In the fifties more than a million British kids queued excitedly outside cinemas for their weekly fix of stirring entertainment. They were boisterous, noisy, and total chaos but what a time we had. The crush started when the doors opened, sixpences were handed over at the kiosk and then came the mad dash into the theatre to get the best seat you could.

The large cinema chains had children's clubs, the Granada Grenadiers, the Century Rangers, or like mine, the ABC Minors.

The show usually started with a song, which everyone joined in enthusiastically.
Ours went something like this:

We are the boys and girls well known as
Minors of the ABC (ABC was shouted at the top of our voices)
And every Saturday all line up
To see the films we like and shout aloud with glee
We like to laugh and have our sing-song
Such a happy crowd are we ee!
We're all pals together
We're Minors of the ABC

After the club song there were competitions, talent shows, presentations to those with a birthday, and then of course the films. These usually began with cartoons, followed by the feature film, and finally, an episode of the serial.
It was barely controlled mayhem as hundreds of shrill voices cheered for their heroes and booed the baddies. The adventures of the Lone Ranger, Flash Gordon, or Zorro always ended with a cliff hanger to make sure we came back next week - not that there was much chance we wouldn't.
On the way home we became our screen heroes; macs buttoned up at the neck became our capes and any suitable twig became the 'Sword of Zorro.'
Happy days indeed!

Going to the Pub

One of Britain's most popular pastimes, certainly among men, was a visit to the good old British pub.
The main room of a 1950s pub was the public bar. Full of smoke and bad language, this was a male domain where the most popular drink was mild, which cost 9d a pint in 1955. Some drinkers liked to liven their mild up by mixing a half with a bottle of brown ale. This was a 'brown and mild', a 'mixed', or 'a pint of twos', depending on which part of the country you were in.

The presence of females in the bar was frowned upon, but some pubs had a smaller, more intimate room called the snug, which was more welcoming to women. As the fifties progressed, our pubs even began to actively encourage the ladies to visit, with new drinks like Babycham and CherryB to entice them in. In 1957 Babycham became the first alcoholic drink to be advertised on British television. It almost single-handedly changed the nation's drinking culture by marketing itself directly at women, targeting them with their first specific 'ladies" drink, complete with its cute little deer logo.

1957

October 10, 1957

The Flu Scourge

This Asian Flu is tearing through the land.
As our ancestors did when the "black death" was
abroad, we count our colleagues each morning
and wonder who will be knocked out next.

October 14, 1957

The Space Age Has Arrived

Today is the eleventh day of Space Year One.
The new age that started when Russia took man's
centuries old dream of space travel off the draw-
ing board and sent the Sputnik bleeping round
the globe.
Within two years, according to Russian scientists,
a permanent satellite circling the Earth will be
commonplace and there will be a satellite girdling
the moon.

Special Occasions
****

Bonfire Night

On 5th November, 1605, Guy Fawkes was found in the cellars underneath Parliament, which were found to contain a large number barrels of gunpowder hidden under piles of coal and firewood. It transpired that Fawkes was part of a Catholic plot to assassinate the Protestant King James and replace him with a Catholic king.
In the aftermath, Parliament declared November 5, a national day of thanksgiving for the King's deliverance and passed a law that made it compulsory to celebrate the occasion. Although the act was dissolved in 1859, we had become rather attached to our quirky, uniquely British custom, and we have been celebrating it ever since, although the way we celebrate has changed over time. Today, the bonfires and fireworks displays we attend are mainly the organised events.

We just buy a ticket and turn up to watch the show, but in the fifties, certainly where I lived, it was a much more do it yourself affair. It started about a month before the actual night, when the neighbourhood kids, the gang, began scouring the district for material to build the bonfire, but that wasn't as easy as it might sound. You see, the gang down the road were doing exactly the same thing and competition for good combustible material was fierce. It wasn't uncommon for fisticuffs to break out if both groups at the same time discovered something that might burn. Worse than that though was the pilfering. You could get close to building the perfect bonfire only to find, the following day, that half of it had been stolen. We would then mount a counter raid on our rival's bonfire, and so it went on. Somehow it always seemed to work out and both sides managed to build a decent bonfire, so I suppose it was all a waste of time really, but it kept us out of mischief.

When we weren't waging the Battle of the Bonfires, we busied ourselves making a guy, which we hoped would help raise a few pennies for the fireworks fund. We pushed it round the neighbourhood in an old pram shouting "penny for the guy" at anyone who appeared, or even knocking on people's doors. We usually raised enough with our guy to buy some penny bangers from Ravenhill's, or should I say, acquire some bangers. In the fifties it was illegal to sell fireworks to anyone under the age of 13, but it was always possible to persuade or bribe someone old enough to get them for you.

So, armed with our stash of explosives, we set off to cause some pre-bonfire night mayhem in the streets. I know, I know, it's appalling behaviour, and I should be ashamed of myself, but if it's any consolation, as I wrote this part, I was thinking what an idiot I was, but I was young, and young people sometimes do stupid things. When it came to the big night itself the adults took over, lighting the bonfire and setting off the real fireworks. Rockets were the best, launched from milk bottles. Catherine Wheels promised a lot but somehow didn't always live up to it.

When the fireworks were done it was time for food. Wonderful homemade toffee apples, and my favourite, potatoes that had been baking in the fire.

They were always caked in brittle charcoal and way
overcooked but, with a bit of salt and a knob of butter,
they were delicious, and you could tell who'd eaten one
because there was a black ring around their mouth.
So, with full stomachs and reeking of smoke it was all
over for another year, well, not quite. There were plenty
of spent rockets to search for tomorrow.

A 1950s Christmas

A 1950s Christmas, in essence, was the same as today.
It was about families getting together, swapping gifts,
eating way too much, and stretching the family budget.
One big difference though, was that the budget wasn't
stretched beyond the means of the family. Credit cards
didn't exist in the fifties, so Christmas on credit just
wasn't an option. Most households tried to put away a
little bit each week and spend only what they had managed to save.

For children, one of the first signs that Christmas was getting closer was making paper chains at school from loops of brightly coloured paper to decorate the classroom.

When you got home, you might detect the smell of Christmas pudding emanating from the wash copper as it slowly cooked, things were hotting up in more ways than one.

The highlight of the build up to Christmas for me was the annual bus ride into the city with my mum to visit Father Christmas's Grotto in Lewis's department store.

There was always a long queue of excited children, and far from excited, albeit resigned parents, waiting for a one on one with Father Christmas, but that was fine, for me anyway, because there were amazing, animated, Christmas displays along the way to keep me entertained.

In the fifties, the tree was rarely put up more than a week before Christmas Day, and in many households as late as Christmas Eve, so when it appeared, we knew the big day was nearly upon us.

The Christmas activity reached a frenzied peak on Christmas Eve. Few homes had fridges back then, so the festive food had to be bought as close to the big day as possible. All over Britain, housewives, and any other family members they could rope in, headed to butchers, grocers, greengrocers, and bakers to collect their orders, then trudge home laden with Christmas fare.

Then there were sprouts and spuds to peel, peas to shell – my favourite task as I could scoff a few in the process – and chickens or ducks to stuff, or possibly an expensive Turkey if you could afford it.

Once a glass of sherry had been placed where Father Christmas couldn't miss it, and a carrot left on the doorstep for Rudolph, it was time for bed. But you're never going to get to sleep are you? You're way too excited, and if you stay awake you might even catch a glimpse of Father Christmas. But sleep overtakes you and the next thing you know you're waking up, and there, next to the bed, as if by magic, is a Christmas stocking. This could be a pillow case, large sock, or, in my case, one of my mum's cast off nylon stockings, stuffed with a variety of goodies. There was always some sweets and chocolate (sweet rationing had ended by the time my memories of Christmas begin) and I munched away while I explored the rest of the stocking's many contents.

All I can remember now though is a satsuma and some shiny new coins, and I suspect I'm not alone in that. When I had finished with the stocking, I had to wait impatiently to be allowed downstairs to open my proper presents, which sat enticingly under the tree.

Beano and Bunty annuals, jig-saws, dolls and plastic tea sets, Airfix models and Meccano sets were popular children's gifts in the 1950s, and if you were really, really lucky, a gleaming new bike.

While the kids played with their new toys, mum got on with dinner, and before you knew it, there it was, laid out on the table, steaming hot and looking delicious. There might even be some pop for the kids, a Babycham for mum, and a bottle of beer for dad, and if they really wanted to be daring, an exotic bottle of wine from the outdoor. The highlight of the Christmas dinner, for me anyway, was the pudding, and not just eating it, but the whole ceremony surrounding it.

My dad's main contribution to the day, apart from paying for it all, was setting fire to the Christmas pud. He would disappear into the outhouse, the lights were dimmed, and he would reappear bearing a flaming pudding.

When the flames had subsided, the steaming ball was dished out and smothered with custard, and then – well, I'd like to say that I tucked in, but that isn't actually true. You see, I knew that somewhere in it was a sixpence and I didn't really want to choke on Christmas Day, so I sifted through it carefully, taking very small spoonful's that I was sure weren't dangerous.

Although the pudding was always delicious, the sifting process slightly spoiled the experience and, to make things worse, I don't ever remember finding the sixpence.

Dinner was finished and cleared away in time to listen to the Royal Christmas Message at three o'clock in the afternoon, absolutely essential in most 1950s households.

The Royal Christmas message was first broadcast on radio by King George V in 1932. His granddaughter Elizabeth II gave her first message in 1952 and set a precedent in 1957 when it was shown on television for the first time.

In the fifties, Christmas wasn't the extended holiday we enjoy today, certainly not for those with jobs. Factory and office workers might finish early on Christmas Eve, have Christmas Day and Boxing Day off, and be back at work the following day. The longer summer holiday seemed a long way off.

Holiday Time

The second world war had seriously disrupted the great British seaside holiday but, by 1950, the lure of the seaside was pulling people back, and our traditional resorts were again attracting the crowds.

West Sussex Gazette August 10, 1950
Southsea had its busiest Bank Holiday weekend since before the war and the front was thronged with thousands of holidaymakers on each day. Traffic on the railways created a post-war record.

A 1950s holiday though, was a far cry from what we might expect today. The equivalent of a flight to Benidorm was a train ride to Blackpool, Bridlington, or Brighton for a week in the sun, or the wind and rain, or whatever else the British summertime could throw at us.

But would the weather spoil our fun? Not on your nelly, it was our holiday, and we were determined to enjoy it. Many industrial towns had local holiday weeks, called Wakes Weeks, when all the factories closed, and the workers all took their holidays at the same time. This sparked a mass exodus with thousands of families heading for the seaside, leaving ghost towns behind.

People from the Lancashire mill towns went to Blackpool or Morecambe, Yorkshire families, Scarborough or Filey, Midlanders to Weston-super-Mare, and Londoners flocked to Brighton or Margate.

For most working-class families, hotels were too expensive and the good old, down to earth, boarding house was the accommodation of choice.

Full board in a Blackpool boarding house would set you back 12/6 a night in 1950, although in those days it was quite normal for guests to take their own food, which the landlady would cook for them.

Beyond the boarding house there was a whole world of pleasure to explore.

There were amusement arcades and fun fairs, stalls selling cockles and whelks, fish and chip shops galore, and shops selling sticks of rock, postcards, buckets and spades, plastic windmills, and little flags to decorate your sandcastle.

Along the front were little shelters where you could sit and watch the world go by, and then, there was the beach.

A popular British beach in holiday season was something to behold. Brightly coloured deck chairs, kids building sandcastles and splashing in the sea, donkey rides, swing boats, and Punch and Judy shows, and if it was a bit chilly, we just put on our coats and got on with it.

There were also sights that would cause some amusement today, but in the fifties would hardly cause a second glance.

A man sunbathing in a suit with a hanky on his head for example, or paddling in the sea with suit trousers rolled up, were perfectly normal, as long as you were British of course.

My nan often joined us on our family holidays and on this one, at Weston-Super-Mare, she seems to be having as much fun as I did. She must have been feeling very daring to go barefoot in public, although she drew the line when it came to taking off her hat and cardie.

Butlins

The traditional British seaside holiday was an institution, but some were trying to change the way we holidayed. Billy Butlin opened his first holiday camp in Skegness in 1936 and a second in Clacton two years later.

The outbreak of war in 1939 curtailed his grand plans and the Skegness and Clacton camps were given over to military use.

After the war he picked up where he left off, and by 1950, Butlins was offering an alternative to the typical bucket and a spade holiday.

A week at a Butlins holiday camp in August 1950 would set you back £7 17shillings and 6 pence.

Each family had their own small chalet, and were greeted every morning by a cheery announcement on the public address system, "Good morning campers, this is Radio Butlins."

Youngsters could join the
Butlins Beavers, there were
all manner of activities to
keep the family busy dur-
ing the day, and there was
entertainment every night,
all organised by an army of
cheerful redcoats who were
always around to make
sure you had a good time,
whether you wanted to or
not.

A Working Holiday

There were many families in 1950s Britain that couldn't afford a holiday of any kind, but some enterprising folk found a way round it.

Every summer, more than a hundred thousand Eastenders left London to go hop picking in Kent and Sussex for a holiday with pay.

Many of the pickers went to the same place year after year, taking children with them who continued the tradtion for generations.

Basic accommodation was provided and the work was hard, with the whole family joining in, but it was still a wonderful opportunity to escape the smoke and grime of the city and, for many East End kids, the chance to see cows for the first time. It was a far cry from Butlins but most of the hop pickers look back at their working holidays in Kent fondly.

1958

21 Die in Soccer Plane Crash

Seven Manchester United footballers were among 21 people killed when their chartered airliner crashed and burst into flame in Munich today.

Ten United players and their famous manager, Matt Busby, were injured, some critically.

The airliner was bringing the United party back from Belgrade where they drew 3-3 with Red Star in a European Cup game yesterday.

After stopping at Munich to refuel the pilots of the plane had already made two attempts to take off but, due to heavy snow, had been unable to gain the necessary power.

On the third attempt the plane raced along the runway and again refused to rise but this time it was too late to pull up. At 200 m.p.h. it crashed into a two-storey wooden house and an adjoining cottage some 300 yards beyond the runway and burst into flames.

September 10, 1958

Cod War Sailors Use Spuds as Ammo!

The cod war off Iceland became a fish-and-chip war yesterday.

The first salvo was fired by the crew of the Icelandic gun boat Odin. As the British trawler Loch Fleet sailed by, lumps of dried cod flew from the Odin's deck.

Earlier a spud and broom handle engagement had been fought between the British trawler Stella Caponus and Iceland's gunboat, Maria Julia. Maria closed on Stella. "Repel boarders" roared Stella's skipper Jim Osborne.

Maria was pushed off by the trawler's crew with broom handles and the galley staff joined in with a stock of mouldy potatoes and hits were scored on the Icelandic crew.

Maria Julia moved off but as she did so, her crew shouted menacingly that they'd be back.

Communication
****

Keeping in Touch

While more and more British households had a TV set, very few were yet to acquire a telephone. In 1955 they could be found in only 14% of homes. The rest of us had to make do with the public phones in the bright red boxes that were prolific in built up areas. It wasn't at all unusual to have to wait in a queue to make your call, or to have someone banging on the door impatiently if they thought your turn was taking too long, or perhaps they were actually waiting for a call. Each telephone box had its own phone number and it wasn't uncommon for people to converse from one phone box to another. This of course had to be prearranged so it was very frustrating if one of the boxes happened to be occupied. You also had to make sure you had the right coins because there were no card payments in the 1950s.

Do you remember the buttons? A if your call was answered and B to get your money back if not. It was very important as a child, when passing an empty phone box, not to forget to press button B to see if the last caller had forgotten to retrieve their unused coins.

Thruppence bought a lot of sweets back then! The mobile phone age brought about the steady decline of the public pay phone, but the red phone box is now hailed as a British design icon and original boxes can change  hands for as much as £3000. Others have been put to a variety of imaginative uses, such as free libraries and defibrillator stations, even miniature coffe shops.

The main way people kept in touch in the fifties was by post, which by today's standards, seems positively archaic. In the fifties there were two deliveries each weekday and one on Saturday, so, let's say you decided on Monday you wanted to meet a friend on Friday. You could send a letter on Monday, get a reply on Tuesday, and send another letter to confirm that you had received her reply. What a palaver compared to what we've got used to. A quick call or exchange of messages and it's all sorted in a few minutes.

In the fifties, if you needed to contact someone urgently, for most people, the only option was to send a telegram.

This meant contacting a Post Office which, as few people had phones, was usually done in person.

You gave your message and the delivery address to a member of staff at the Post Office, who typed it into a teleprinter. Charges were based on the numbr of words so messages were kept as brief as possible. The message was sent to the Central Telegraph Office who forwarded it to the destination Post Office. There, a navy blue uniformed Telegram boy was despatched on a bicycle or motor cycle with a printed copy for delivery to the final recipient. A priority telegram would usually be delivered within the hour.

Travel

In the 1950s, for most people, taking on a journey longer than your feet, bicycle, or the bus could carry you presented quite a challenge.

It wasn't a problem most of the time because, back then, people tended not to venture far from home. The exception was at holiday time. For most of us, certainly in the first half of the decade, getting to the seaside involved a train journey, which required planning, stamina, and a great deal of patience.

The operation usually started with a bus journey to the station, which was far from straightforward with excited kids in tow and suitcases to carry. They didn't have wheels in those days – the cases not the kids!

Evolution hasn't taken us that far - not yet anyway.

You eventually get everybody and everything on to the bus, with a bit of help from the conductor if you're lucky. Do you remember bus conductors with their ticket machines round their necks?

We got on to buses at the back then by an open platform with a vertical pole in the middle, remember that? Wasn't it daring to jump off while the bus was still moving?

Everybody piles off the bus at the railway station where the scene is one of absolute pandemonium; this is Saturday morning at the height of the British holiday season after all.

The first thing to do is find the ticket office where you join the long queue (no such thing as e-tickets in the fifties) but you were prepared for this, and you've allowed plenty of time.

You've managed to save enough money through the year to buy second-class tickets. The other options are third-class, which is not as comfortable, or first-class, which is too expensive. Mind you, even if you had the money for first-class, you wouldn't choose it. That would be frivolous, which was frowned upon in the 1950s.

With tickets secured, the family makes its way to the designated platform to join hundreds of other holiday makers heading for the same destination.

Here you're greeted by the awesome sight and sound of the steam locomotive, huffing, and snorting and puffing, impatient to whisk us off to our holiday paradise – or Blackpool would be fine.

To add to the romance of these steaming monsters, many of them carried grand sounding names; The Great Marquis, The Brighton Belle, The William Shakespeare, and probably the most famous of them all, The Flying Scotsman. No wonder so many kids went train spotting in the fifties.

It's a bit of a struggle getting the suitcases through the carriage's narrow doorway, but you eventually get them stashed on the luggage shelf above the upholstered bench seat, and you all settle down for the journey. If you are really lucky you might have the compartment to yourselves but, in the busy holiday period, you will almost certainly be sharing with others.

With a blow of the guard's whistle and a mighty hiss, the train begins to pull away, chugging slowly at first then picking up speed until the sound of the locomotive becomes a rhythmic chuffing, punctuated now and again by the shrill noise of the steam whistle.

In no time you've left the urban sprawl behind, and green fields with sheep and cows grazing are whizzing past the window, obscured occasionally by billowing steam. You're fortunate to have a standard train as op-posed to a holiday special, which means you have a cor-ridor to stretch your legs, and a toilet should you need it. This is the 1950s so there's no digital display telling you what the next station is. You won't know until you get there, but with the aid of a map you can work out roughly how long it will take to get to your destination – and it helps to pass the time. We know when we're getting close, and all eyes focus outwards hoping for that first glimpse of the sea. Finally, with a cacophony of huffs, puffs, chugs, whistles, and a screech of brakes, we have arrived, although getting off the train isn't entirely straightforward is it. You have to pull the leather strap to open the window then lean out to open the door from the outside. This is a rudimentary safety feature to pre-vent passengers from accidentally falling from the train while it's moving. With all the doors successfully opened, the entire human contents of the train, together with their luggage, spew onto the platform and the chaos begins all over again. When you eventually get to your guesthouse you need a holiday to get over the journey.

Third class carriages were introduced in the 1830s to provide a way for the lower classes to travel cheaply, a move bitterly opposed by the upper classes who argued; "if you let the working classes go where they please, who knows what troubles they will stir up, what airs they will start to assume?"

But, just to annoy them, we did go where we pleased, perhaps we did sometimes stir up a little trouble, maybe even assumed some airs, but cheap third-class fares quickly proved popular, and made possible the institution of the family seaside holiday and the growth of the suburbs of every town and city in the country.

Mind you, in the early days, it wasn't a cosy experience by any means. This advice was given to third class passengers in the mid-19th century.

"I advise passengers to get as far from the engine as possible as the vibration is very much diminished. Always sit (if you can get a seat) with your back towards the engine, against the boarded part of the waggon; by this plan you will avoid being chilled by the current of cold air which passes through these open waggons and also save yourself from being blinded by the small cinders which escape from the funnel."

By the fifties, travelling third class was considerably more comfortable, so much so that there was little difference between third and second class, and it was done away with altogether in 1956.

The Motor Car Age

As the decade chugged along, more and more Britons were ending their reliance on the railways and investing in their own rolling stock. Yes, they were buying their first motor car.

In 1950, only about 14% of households had the use of a car, and most of those were in wealthy areas. In poor neighbourhoods, the only cars they saw were probably rent collectors or police, and the sight of a horse-drawn cart was more common, but things were beginning to change. As employment grew and wages rose, so did people's aspirations.

Whereas owning a car for most people had been just a dream, a growing sense of well-being had us starting to think, maybe, just maybe!

It often took one person in the neighbourhood to take the plunge to get others thinking, "if George round the corner can do it, why not us?" - even if it was on the never-never.

The most popular car in 1952 was the Morris Minor, which would set you back a princely £631, or the equivalent of 20 months' salary for the average worker.

By the end of the decade car ownership would more than double. But the onset of motoring for the masses wasn't without its growing pains. In 1952, 4700 people were killed in road accidents, that's nearly two and a half times the average yearly total now, even though there are an extra 30 million cars on the road. In 1951, in an effort to bring some order to our increasingly busy roads, zebra crossings were introduced to give pedestrians precedence over all other traffic.

It would be almost a decade though before another serious safety issue was addressed. A lot of the vehicles on our roads were bought second hand, with many of them manufactured before 1940. There was no legal requirement to have these vehicles safety checked and there were thousands of cars on the road that were potentially dangerous. It wasn't until 1960 that compulsory MOT testing was introduced for vehicles over 10 years old. A lot of people died in the meantime.

But, there was no slowing the galloping pace of the motor car age. By the end of the 1950s, car ownership had more than doubled, and it was easy to see why, take holidays for example. No more lugging suitcases to the bus stop, wrestling them on to the train, and sharing a compartment with complete strangers; your own personal carriage awaited, right outside the house.

Load up the luggage, stuff the kids in the back with a few toys, make sure you've got the directions you scribbled down last night, and with a turn of the key you're off to the seaside. But it wasn't that simple was it, because we were also getting accustomed to a new phenomenon, the traffic jam.

So, you haven't moved for ten minutes, the car's overheating, and so is dad, mum is trying in vain to keep the kids amused, you're trapped in this hot metal box, and there's not even a corridor where you can stretch your legs or use the loo.

"Perhaps we should have taken the train dear."

"AARGH!"

Still, at least you'd had the foresight to join the AA, just in case - there's a badge on the front of the car to prove it - and in the glove box is a key to open the AA road-side phone boxes if you need their help.

Automobile Association patrol men were a common site on the roads, dressed in brown uniforms and usually on motorbikes with yellow side-cars.

If a patrol man saw a vehicle bearing the AA badge coming in the other direction, he would salute the driver. If he didn't, it was wise to slow down because the absence of a salute could be a covert warning of a police speed trap round the corner.

By the middle of the decade, it was obvious that roads originally built for stagecoaches simply couldn't handle the volume of traffic now trying to squeeze on to them. A radical solution was required if Britain could deal with a new age in transport.

A new era for travel in Britain began when the first stage of the M6 motorway, the Preston by-pass, opened on December 5th, 1958.

Unfortunately, the new road seemed initially to have defeated its own object as thousands of sight-seeing motorists, eager to take a test drive, jammed the approach roads to the by-pass.

The following year the M1 opened to become the first full-length motorway in the UK, with Watford Gap, Britain's first motorway services.

Our First Car

I remember coming home from school one day and seeing a car parked outside our house, which was very odd.
Our road was a dead end and the only vehicles that used
it belonged to delivery men and the dustman. I went into
the house, concerned that the appearance of the strange
car was a sign that something was wrong. My concern increased when I saw my dad standing in the kitchen next
to my mum – he was never there when I got home. My
fears subsided however when I realised they both had
half smiles on their faces, and the reason was revealed
when I asked why there was a car outside. It was ours.
I couldn't believe it, we had a car, a big (to me anyway)
green, shiny one, called an Austin Devon.

It wasn't new of
course, but it was
beautiful, and it
changed my young
life. Weekends were
now about drives in
the countryside and
picnics in
wonderful places

I couldn't even imagine existed before. Habberley Valley,
Evesham, Bidford on Avon, became part of my childhood memories thanks to our Austin Devon. I still had
to visit my nan on Sunday, but now it was usually to pick
her up to join us on a new countryside adventure.

So, my family and I had joined that growing army of Britons called motorists. We were a nation on the move, speeding, headlong down our brand new motorways towards a new decade.

The Swinging Sixties would come to overshadow the fifties in popular culture, but without the developments of the 1950s, the youth revolution especially, the sixties wouldn't have been anywhere near as swinging.
And we can say, my fellow baby boomers and I, that we were there, and, although we didn't know it at the time, we played our part in changing Britain for ever.

The photos of our decade might be in monotone, but everyday life back then was far from it. It was colourful and vibrant, not always easy admittedly, but just so interesting - I mean, can you imagine a child of today, in decades to come, reminiscing nostalgically about dad turning up the central heating, or mum loading the washing machine?
No, nor me!

We will continue to look back at the fifties with fondness, sometimes through rose-coloured spectacles maybe, but who cares, I think we've earned the right to be a little self-indulgent in our dotage, don't you?

Anyway, the Archers has just finished so I'm off to bed. Nighty night!

IN THE NEWS
1959

15,000 Come Marching In

The Ban the H-Bomb procession was seven miles long by the time the marchers reached Trafalgar Square yesterday. Even officials of the Campaign for Nuclear Disarmament which organised the four day trek from the Atomic Weapons Research Establishment at Aldermaston were astounded at the final turnout.

Farewell to the Fifties

Ten years that changed the world .... that was the 1950s. It was the decade when the 20th century really began, and life will never be the same again. The fifties will be recalled as a period in which television came to exert its powerful influence, and in which we took to the roads in motorised hordes, slaughtered each other in thousands and faced up to the truth that mass motoring means mass congestion. Despite this however, I believe we can look forward to the sixties with hope and trust.

A Final Word (Almost)

Firstly, thank you for reading this book, I hope you enjoyed it and that it brought back some memories of your own from the 1950s.

If, like me, your childhood and early teenage memories are spread across the 50s and 60s, you might be interested to know that I am now working on Looking Back at the 1960s.

If you think you would like to read this also, keep an eye open for its launch on Amazon, or, let us know your email address and we will notify you directly of its release. You can contact me at dave@britainonfilm.co.uk.

I would also be very interested to hear your own personal memories of the 1960s.

Please send them to the email address above.

Thanks again and I look forward to hearing from you.

And, finally, don't forget to take the Eleven Plus.

Re-sit the Eleven Plus

GENERAL ENGLISH

1. Make adjectives from these nouns: beauty, slope, glass, friend, doubt, expense, delight, sleep, danger, sport.

2. Write these lines of poetry in the usual way, putting in capital letters and the correct punctuation: the evening is coming the sun sinks to rest the rooks are all flying straight home to the nest caw says the rook, as he flies overhead it's time little people were going to bed.

3. Choose the correct word from those in brackets:
a) She gave the (fare, fair) to the conductor.
b) I am (confidant, confident) of success.
c) Why does she (die, dye) her hair?
d) His sister has (wrote, written) him a letter.
e) The screw fell off because it was (lose, loose).

4. Fill in the relative pronoun in the following sentences:
a) That is the coat .... my brother took away.
b) The man to .... I spoke was very disagreeable.
c) The boy .... ball I kicked was offended.
d) The man .... does his duty is always brave.
e) He asked me .... I intended to do.

5. Each of the following sentences contains one error.
Re-write the sentences correctly:

a) This is not an Infant's School.
b) I am told that Tom Jones's brother have won a scholarship
c) The bishop and another fellow then entered the hall.
d) When the dog recognised me it wagged it's tail.
e) The matter does not concern you or I.
f) Talking to my friend, the bus passed me.

COMPREHENSION
Read the following:

'You are old, Father William,' the young man said, 'And
your hair has become very white; And yet you incessantly stand on your head - Do you think, at your age, it is
right?'
'In my youth,' Father William replied to his son, 'I feared
it might injure the brain; 'But, now that I'm perfectly
sure I have none, 'Why, I do it again and again.'
'You are old,' said the youth, 'as I mentioned before,
'And have grown most uncommonly fat;
'Yet you turned a back-somersault in at the door - 'Pray,
what is the reason of that?' 'In my youth,' said the sage,
as he shook his grey locks, 'I kept all my limbs very supple.
'By the use of this ointment - one shilling the box -
'Allow me to send you a couple?'

146

Now answer these questions:

a) Father William was certainly a queer man. Mention two queer things that he did.

b) When he was young, Father William thought that one of his pranks might do him harm. When he was old, he changed his mind. Why?

c) What does 'incessantly' mean? What is a back-somersault?

d) What does the word 'supple' mean? How did Father William keep supple? Do you keep supple in the same way?

e) What signs of old age did Father William show?

ARITHMETIC

Read the following:

1. 3,755 is multiplied by 25 and the result is divided by 125. Write down the answer.

2. A motorist leaves home at 10.15am and drives at 32 miles per hour. He stops for lunch from noon to 1.45pm and then continues his journey at 30 miles per hour. How many miles has he travelled by 5pm?

3. An aeroplane uses 100 gallons of petrol for a flight of 150 miles. How far could it fly using 40 gallons?

4. Write in figures: twelve thousand and twelve.

5. A race started at 23 minutes past three and finished at 23 minutes to four. How long did it take?

6. Simplify:
a) 1,000 - 10
b) 25 x 12
c) 615 divided by 3
d) 0.5 + 0.75
e) The fractions 4/5 - 7/10
7. Of 800 people living in a village, half are men and half women. A quarter of the men leave the village to join the army. How many more women then men now remain?
8. Multiply 7,296 by 479.
9. Which of these numbers is divisible by 4 without any remainder: 214, 230, 226, 224, 218?
10. Add all the odd numbers between 12 and 20.

GENERAL INTELLIGENCE/KNOWLEDGE

Read the following:
1. The letters ERBDA are just the letters of the word BREAD mixed up. Now, straighten up the following:

a) AAANNB is a fruit which comes from abroad.
b) ROHES is a large animal.
c) GRATEAMR is a girl's name.
d) DWEBORRA is an article of furniture.
e) SAIRINS are used in Christmas puddings.

2. Select and write down one of the answers below which makes the best answer to the following:
A woman who had fallen into the water was dragged out in a drowning condition by a man, but she did not thank him because:
a) She never felt thankful for small things.
b) She did not know the man well enough.
c) She was feeling better.
d) She was still unconscious.

3. Complete the following by giving words expressing sound and ending in 'ing'.
e.g. the humming of telephone wires.
a) the .... of leaves
b) the .... of anvils.
c) the .... of brakes.
d) the .... of stairs.

4. In each of the sets of words given below there is one word meaning something rather different from the other three. Find the different word in each line and write it down:
a) alike, same, similar, somewhat.
b) pigeon, duck, goose, swan.
c) bus, conductor, passenger, driver.
d) this, that, the, those.
e) firm, rough, solid, hard.
f) desk, book, cupboard, drawer.
g) spade, earth, sand, gravel.

h) pretty, nice, charm, lovely.

i) justice, merciful, pitying, forgiving.

j) tumbler, cup, mug, jug.

k) fishing, rowing, climbing, swimming.

l) scarlet, blue, red, pink.

m) sewing, cotton, needle, calico.

5. Each of the following sentences here can be made into better sense by interchanging two words.

Re-write the sentences correctly: E.g. Milk like cats - Cats like milk.

a) Our black cat had a retriever with the fight next door.

b) The sea went to the family for a swim.

c) The shepherd whistled by the gate and stood to his dog.

d) A was stung by Joan bee.

e) Sailors have to climb able to be.

The answers start on the next page and remember, no cheating, or else!

70% right and you've passed the Eleven Plus, so that's 52 correct answers.

Eleven Plus Answers

GENERAL ENGLISH

1. beautiful, sloping, glassy, friendly, doubting, expensive, delightful, sleeping, dangerous, sporting/sporty

2. The evening is coming, The sun sinks to rest, The rooks are all flying Straight home to the nest. 'Caw', says the rook, As he flies overhead, 'It's time little people Were going to bed.'

3. a) fare; b) confident; c) dye; d) written; e) loose

4. a) which; b) whom; c) whose;

5. a) This is not an Infants' School.

b) I am told that Tom Jones's brother has won a scholarship.

c) The bishop and another gentleman then entered the hall.

d) When the dog recognised me it wagged its tail.

e) The matter does not concern you or me.

f) While talking to my friend, the bus passed me.

COMPREHENSION

a) Two queer things that Father William did were to stand on his head and turn a back-somersault at the door.

b) Father William changed his mind because he is sure he doesn't have a brain to injure.

c) 'Incessantly' means repeatedly, without relief. A back-somersault is when someone jumps over backwards.

d) The word 'supple' means flexible. Father William kept supple by using an ointment.

e) The signs of old age that Father William showed were white hair and growing fat.

ARITHMETIC

1. 751
2. 153.5 miles
3. 60 miles
4. 12,012
5. 14 minutes
6. a) 990 b) 300 c) 205 d) 1.25 e) 1/10
7. 100 more women
8. 3,494,784
9. 224
10. 64

GENERAL INTELLIGENCE/ KNOWLEDGE

1. a) banana; b) horse; c) Margaret d) wardrobe; e) raisins

2. The best answer would be d)

3. a) rustling; b) banging; c) screeching; d) creaking

4. a) somewhat; b) pigeon; c) bus; d) the; e) rough; f) book; g) spade; h) charm; i) justice; j) jug; k) climbing; l) blue; m) sewing

5. a) Our black cat had a fight with the retriever next door.

b) The family went to the sea for a swim.

c) The shepherd stood by the gate and whistled to his dog.

d) Joan was stung by a bee.

e) Sailors have to be able to climb.